W9-CXQ-906

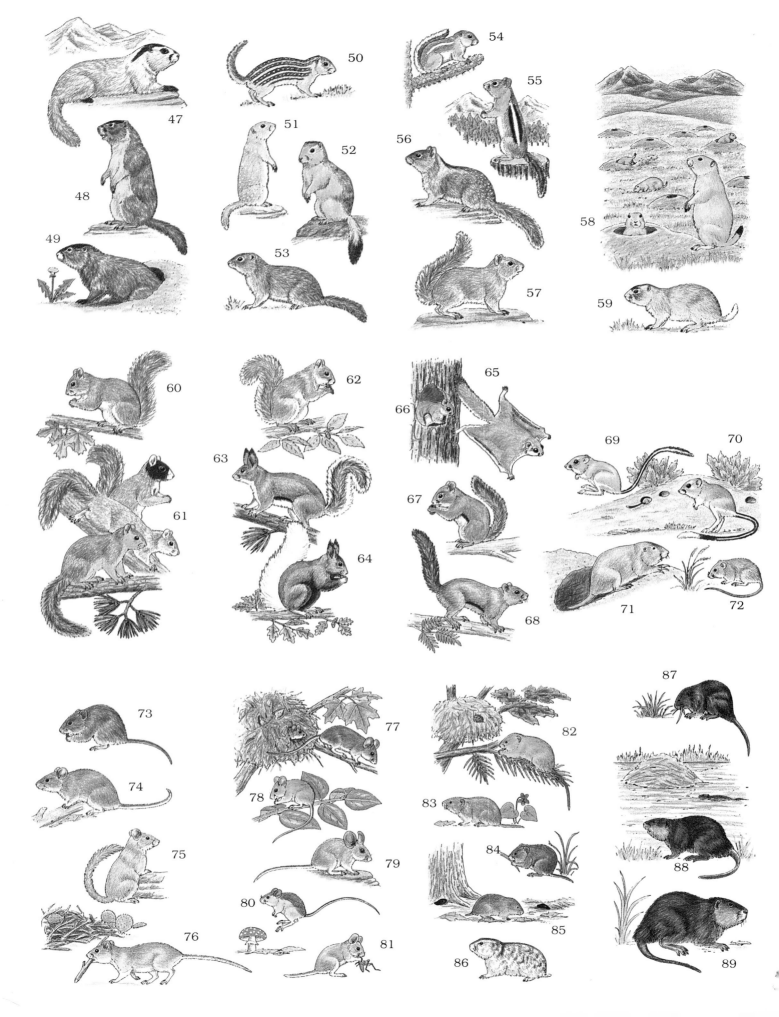

Peterson Field Guide Coloring Books

Mammals

Peter Alden

Illustrated by Fiona Reid

*Sponsored by the
National Wildlife Federation
and the National Audubon Society*

Houghton Mifflin Company   Boston   New York

Printed in the United States of America

HES 15 14 13 12 11 10 9 8 7 6

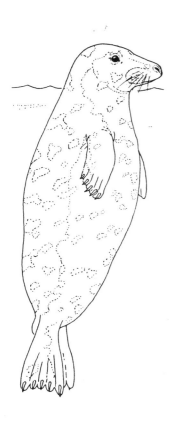

Introduction

Exploring the natural world is a visual activity; it trains the eye. Most budding naturalists soon acquire a copy of one or more of the Peterson Field Guides, such as the *Field Guide to Mammals*. These handy pocket-sized books offer short-cuts to identification, reducing things to basic shapes and patterns, with arrows pointing to the special field marks by which one species can be separated from another.

Although even a person who is colorblind can become skilled at identifying birds or mammals by their shapes and patterns, and flowers and trees by their leaves and other structures, for most of us color is the first clue. The Peterson Field Guide Coloring Books will sharpen your observations and condition your memory for the days you spend outdoors. By filling in the colors during evenings at home or on rainy days, you will be better informed about the animals and plants when you see them in life. Binoculars are a big help if you have a pair; a seven- or eight-power glass makes a bird or mammal seven or eight times as handsome, but it is not necessary for plants, insects, or fishes.

This coloring book will help your color perception and enable you to recognize the common mammals of North America. If you want to learn how to draw, you might try copying the basic line drawings so skillfully prepared by Fiona Reid. You could even try to sketch things in the field, if only roughly in pencil.

Exploring nature can be many things — an art, a science, a game, or a sport — but above all it is an absorbing activity that sharpens the senses, especially the eye and the ear. If you draw or paint, the sense of touch also comes into play; the images of the eye and the mind are transferred by hand to paper. In the process you become more aware of the natural world — the real world — and inevitably you become an environmentalist.

Most of you will find colored pencils best suited for coloring this book, but if you are handy with brushes and paints, you may prefer to fill in the outlines with watercolors. Crayons can also be used. But don't labor; have fun.

Roger Tory Peterson

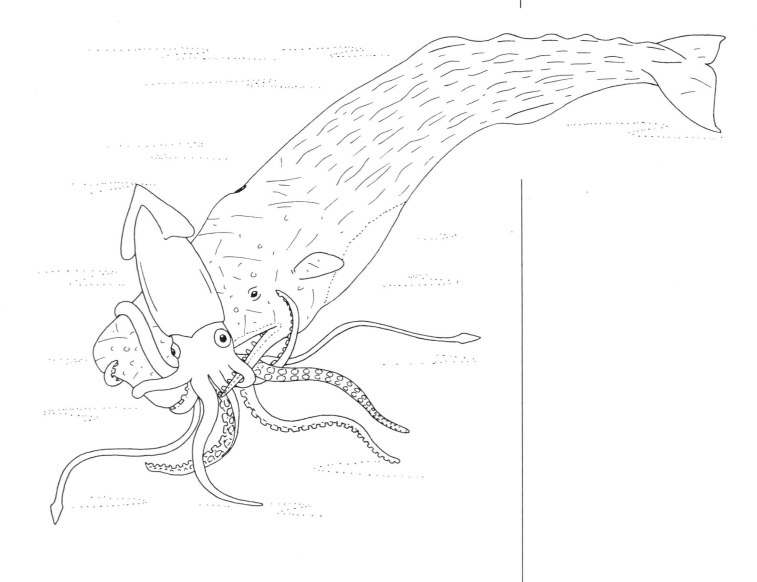

About This Book

Congratulations! You have before you a book that will be fun to color, a proud achievement, and a learning experience. As you carefully color in these outline drawings, use the color paintings on the cover and the descriptions in the text as your guide. You will be absorbing knowledge and developing an interest in seeing these mammals in the wild.

You may wonder why we call these mammals rather than wild animals. Life can be divided into the plant kingdom and the animal kingdom. Within the animal kingdom, there are classes such as insects, fish, reptiles, birds, and mammals. Thus, a Monarch butterfly or a Mourning Dove is an animal, just as a deer is an animal.

Mammals are among Mother Nature's most sophisticated works. You are a mammal, with warm blood, a large brain, and some body hair. Mammals nurture their young on milk, and the young often stay with one or both parents for an extended period. During these weeks, months, or years, the young learn social relations, knowledge of their home territory, tips on food and dangers, and customs from their parents. In lower forms of life, with fewer decisions to make, many of these bits of necessary knowledge are contained in the genes. A young grasshopper knows its options instinctively.

How to Use This Book

Coloring the drawings.   You will get the best results with a large assortment of colored pencils. Obviously, a set with 30 colors, rather than 8, will work much better. Mammals lack the rainbow of colors found on birds, butterflies, and flowers. Nevertheless, you will find a number of shades with which you are not familiar listed as a color on some part of our native mammals. Mammals tend to match the colors of the soil, rocks, and trees; thus, many are brown, gray, black, or white. In the colored drawings, the artist has intensified some of the colors, to highlight contrasting patterns and differences between similar mammals. Some of you may wish to experiment with paints under the guidance of teachers or parents.

Regardless of how perfect your coloring skills, this exercise will imprint on your mind an overwash of fairly accurate colors on a drawing that correctly portrays the shape and pattern of each mammal.

Arrangement.   You may notice that the sequence of mammals included in this book is not based on the alphabet,

size, color, or geography. The mammals of the world are divided into 20 groups called orders. Half of these groups have members that live in North America. The sequence of groups in this book roughly follows an evolutionary time sequence. The first orders of mammals to appear on this planet, such as the marsupials, edentates, and insectivores (see p. 8), are shown and described first. All of these mammals were formerly more common and widespread and had many early forms that are now extinct. The more recently evolved orders of mammals, such as the carnivores, seals, and hoofed mammals, are shown and described last.

The mammals covered in this book belong to the following orders: marsupials, edentates, insectivores, bats, carnivores, seals, rodents, sirenians, rabbits, hoofed mammals, and whales. Within each order are families containing relatively closely related groups of mammals. For example, the dog family within the carnivore order includes dogs, foxes, coyotes, and wolves, all of which share many characteristics.

Throughout this book, most mammals on the same page are members of the same order or family as the others on the page. Major exceptions are the unique Armadillo and Manatee, which have no close relatives in North America. It is important to learn what kinds of mammals are members of each order and family. When you see a little gray mammal with a long nose and short ears running over some leaves, will you instantly know whether it is a meat-eating shrew or a seed-eating rodent? Are seals, whales, dolphins, and sharks basically the same thing? This book is your key to unraveling many a misconception and uncertainty.

Once you have completed coloring all the mammals in this book, I hope that your interest will be whetted to take a second look at mammals. Was that squirrel a Fox or a Gray? How many mammals can you see in your home town or state? Hopefully you will explore your area's woods, fields, and marshes with an eagerness to carefully observe the behavior and diversity of your local mammals. When your family or school is deciding on a vacation spot, I hope you will vote for a wild area where you will see a variety of new mammals.

How to Find Mammals

Although it is relatively easy to go out and find several dozen kinds of birds or flowers on a nature walk lasting a few hours, the same cannot be said of mammals. Larger mammals have become afraid of human scents and usually disappear quickly when we approach. A number of mammals are active only at night and at dusk and dawn.

Mammals should be appreciated one by one as you encounter them. Sometimes it takes luck, sometimes patience,

but if you are eager to see the dozens of mammals present in your area, you can. During the daytime quiet observers will see a variety by chance and local knowledge. Consider going on a nighttime walk with flashlights or stalking wildlife with a camera. You don't have to be a hunter to search out the hoofed mammals. If you can get to the ocean, inquire about doing a one-day whalewatching cruise. If you move or travel, consider what new mammals you should be alert to see in new places.

Check with your school or town library for additional books such as the *Peterson First Guide to Mammals, A Field Guide to the Mammals of North America, A Field Guide to Animal Tracks,* and other books on mammals. You may wish to learn how to live-trap small mammals, or identify tracks in mud or snow, or check droppings. When in the field you will have the best results if you travel alone or in small, quiet groups with frequent rests, always staying alert. Please be careful to avoid destroying the homes of mammals, or unduly harassing them. Perhaps you could photograph them with a telephoto lens or watch them quietly from a blind.

North American mammals.   The earliest peoples to arrive in North America from Asia did not farm crops, raise livestock, or go to supermarkets and restaurants. They survived by hunting, fishing, and gathering wild nuts, seeds, and vegetables. At that time (about 10,000 years ago) our continent was full of huge mammals such as woolly mammoths, many of which became extinct due to overhunting. With the coming of Europeans and the rifle, the remaining species of large mammals faced new dangers. At the turn of the century concerned citizens organized campaigns and organizations to pressure governments to set aside reserves and enact hunting laws. Today we can see increasing numbers of major mammals in parks and private lands due to the foresight of our ancestors. It is your duty to learn about and love all the animals with whom we share the planet. Participate in events at your nature clubs and centers, and support efforts to preserve wildlife habitat in your community.

A final word.   As I wandered the wilder corners of Concord, Massachusetts, as a child, I got to know deer, raccoons, otters, squirrels, skunks, muskrats, and chipmunks. If I had had this coloring book, I would have taken a greater interest in locating a jumping mouse or identifying the bats. Please be curious about the natural community around you. Each time you see a new mammal, it should be the start of a lifetime friendship.

Peter Alden

Virginia Opossum

MARSUPIALS

Australia's kangaroos and the opossums of the Americas are ancient survivors of an old order of mammals whose young complete their development in a fur-lined pouch.

Virginia Opossum A house cat-sized, grayish white or black mammal with a long pink tail that is black at the base. The Opossum is active at night in trees or on the ground. It searches for fruit, nuts, insects, and small animals. When cornered it will fake death, lie limp, and cause predators to lose interest. (**1**)

EDENTATES

Another old order of mammals that includes armadillos, sloths, and anteaters. These mammals live only in Latin America, except for our armadillo.

Nine-banded Armadillo An Armadillo's body is covered with heavy bony armor and flexible bands that help it twist, turn, or roll up into an incomplete ball. This unusual-looking mammal digs up insects with its strong claws. It has recently spread from Texas east to Florida and north to Missouri. (**2**)

Nine-banded Armadillo

INSECTIVORES

An ancient order of small, energetic mammals with long, pointed snouts and numerous sharp teeth.

Shrews

Shrews are a family of tiny, meat-eating insectivores. They search for insects and worms among dead leaves and along streams.

Least Shrew A small, cinnamon-colored shrew with a short tail. It lives in meadows and marshes of the Southeast north to the Great Lakes. **(3)**

Masked Shrew A grayish brown shrew with a long tail that is brown above and buff below. It is common in moist forests of the North. **(4)**

Short-tailed Shrew A large gray shrew with no visible ears and a short tail. The Short-tail is found east of the Great Plains. It kills mice, worms, and slugs with its poisonous saliva. **(5)**

Water Shrew A remarkable little hunter of fish, frogs, and insects. This shrew swims underwater and can also run across water surfaces. It is found across Canada and southward in our higher mountains. **(6)**

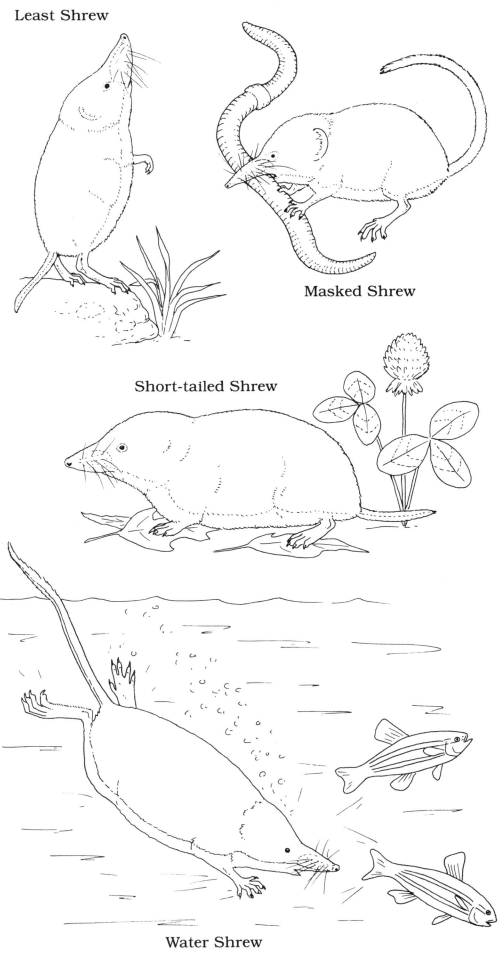

Least Shrew

Masked Shrew

Short-tailed Shrew

Water Shrew

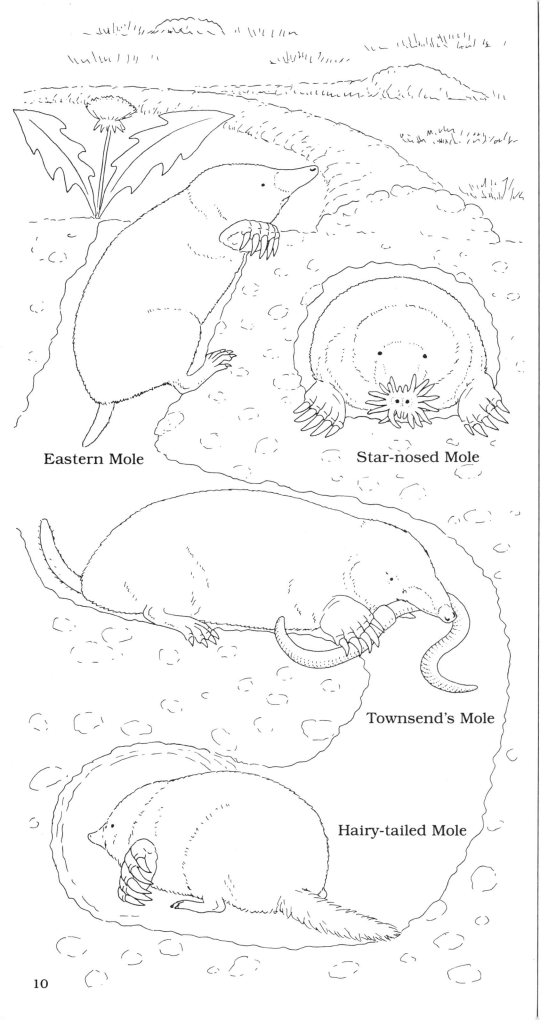

Eastern Mole

Star-nosed Mole

Townsend's Mole

Hairy-tailed Mole

Insectivores: Moles

Moles live mostly under ground. They have spade-like feet with soles that turn outward. Burrowing moles push up ridges on fields and lawns as they search for worms, slugs, and insects. Moles have a long, flexible snout and often show no visible eye. Most moles are grayish black.

Eastern Mole The largest mole of the East and Great Plains. Its tail is pink, naked, and short. This mole is slaty in the North and golden brown in the South. **(7)**

Star-nosed Mole This mole has a fleshy nose that looks like a starfish. The Star-nose often forages above ground and along streams. It lives from the Carolinas north to central Quebec and west to the Dakotas. **(8)**

Townsend's Mole This mole makes its home in the meadows, gardens, and forests of the Pacific states. Its tail is slightly hairy. **(9)**

Hairy-tailed Mole Unlike the others, this mole has a very hairy tail. This mole lives only in the East. **(10)**

BATS

The only mammals that have wings and truly fly. The wings are made of skin that connects the bones of their long arms, hands, and fingers. Bats emit sounds that bounce back, as radar signals do. This helps them locate prey and avoid obstacles in their flight path.

California Leaf-nosed Bat A grayish, long-eared bat of the Southwest with a leaf-like flap on its nose. This bat hovers and swoops down to the ground to catch large insects. **(11)**

Sanborn's Long-nosed Bat A brownish, leaf-nosed bat of the Mexican border country. It feeds on pollen and nectar of flowers. **(12)**

Little Brown Myotis This bat is abundant in large colonies everywhere. Its erratic flight can often be detected before sundown. **(13)**

Hairy-legged Vampire A small brown bat with tiny ears, sharp teeth, and a taste for livestock blood. Rare; found along the Rio Grande valley. **(14)**

Silver-haired Bat This blackish brown bat has silver-tipped hairs on its neck and back. It flies high and straight among trees in northern states and Canada. **(15)**

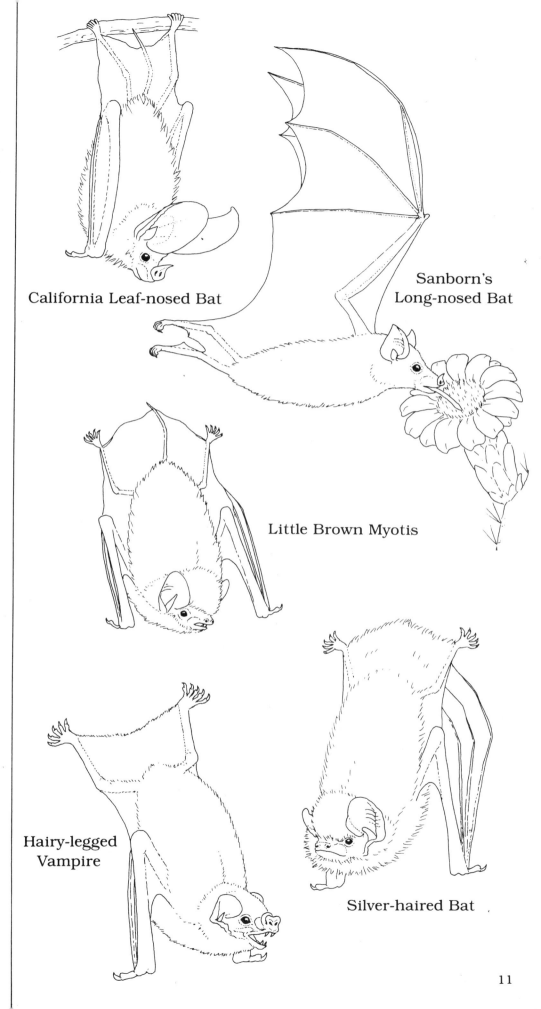

California Leaf-nosed Bat

Sanborn's Long-nosed Bat

Little Brown Myotis

Hairy-legged Vampire

Silver-haired Bat

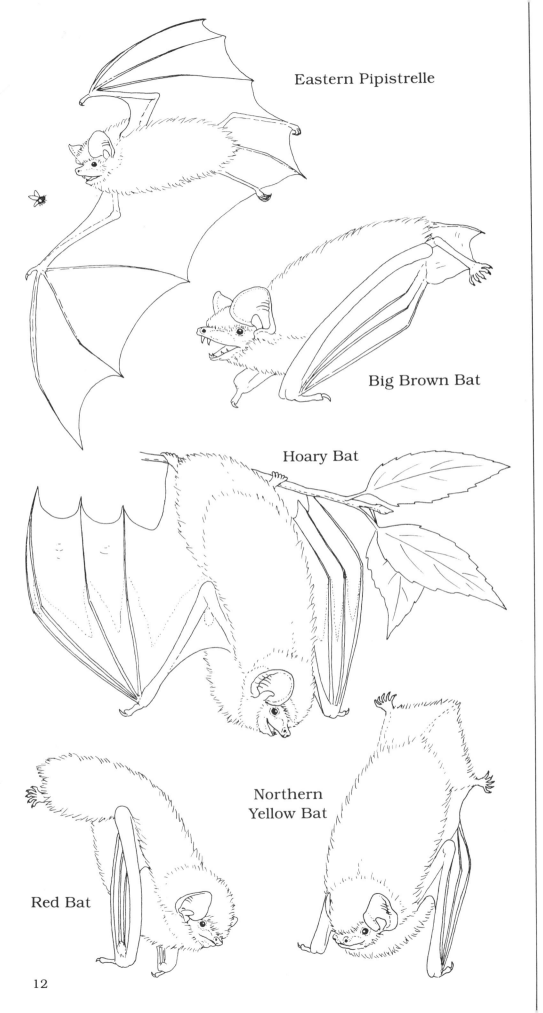

Eastern Pipistrelle

Big Brown Bat

Hoary Bat

Northern Yellow Bat

Red Bat

More Bats

Eastern Pipistrelle The smallest bat in the East, with a length of roughly 5 inches. This light brown or reddish bat flies slowly and erratically as it pursues small insects. (**16**) The **Western Pipistrelle** (not shown) is the smallest bat in the U.S.; it may measure only 4½ inches long. Its color varies from ashy gray to yellowish gray above; the belly is white. Its flight is somewhat jerky. This bat can be seen throughout the Southwest.

Big Brown Bat A large brown bat with black wings. This bat is usually seen by itself rather than in colonies. A fast flier (reaching 40 mph), it chases beetles. (**17**)

Hoary Bat White-tipped hairs cover the brownish body and buffy throat of this bat. It flies high over coniferous forests after sundown. (**18**)

Red Bat Males are bright reddish orange; females are dull red. This bat is found widely except in the Rockies and the deserts. It roosts alone in trees and flies up and down regular courses. The Red Bat is replaced by the Seminole Bat in the Southeast. (**19**)

Northern Yellow Bat A pale yellowish bat of southeastern woodlands from Virginia to Texas. It often roosts in clumps of Spanish moss. (**20**)

More Bats

Spotted Bat   A spectacular dark brown bat with three large white spots above. This bat has huge ears. It lives in arid western regions. **(21)**

Pallid Bat   A very pale bat with large ears. This bat lives in western deserts. It feeds low to the ground, picking up beetles, scorpions, and grasshoppers. **(22)**

Western Mastiff Bat   Our largest bat, almost 11 inches long. It is brown, with a long tail and large ears. Its loud voice can be heard as it echoes from walls of canyons in the Southwest. **(23)**

Brazilian Free-tailed Bat   Also known as the Mexican Freetail. This bat lives in huge colonies throughout the South and Southwest. Some caves in Texas and New Mexico are home to millions. The vast clouds of bats exiting at dusk are now a tourist attraction. The bats feed on moths and insects, and sometimes range many miles from their roosts before returning at dawn. **(24)**

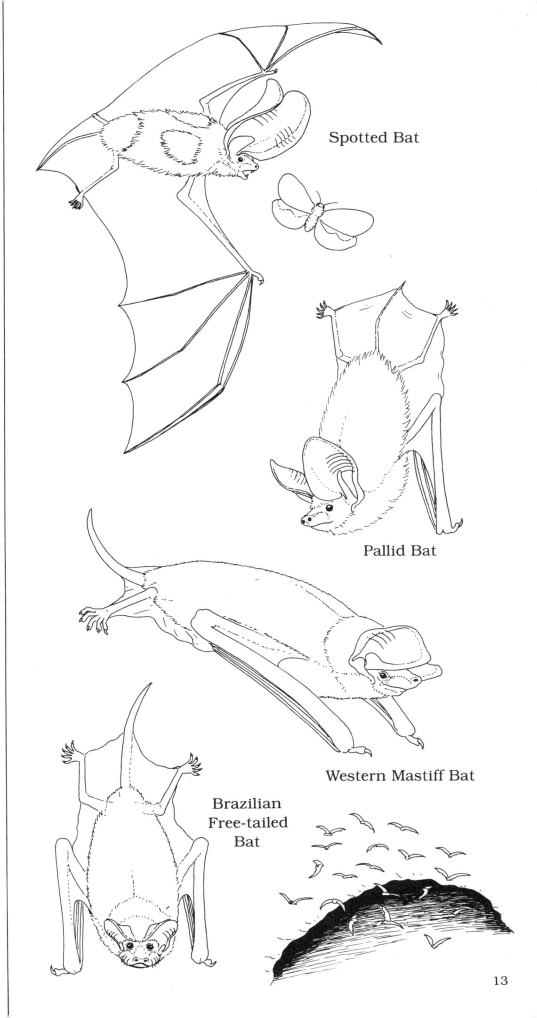

Spotted Bat

Pallid Bat

Western Mastiff Bat

Brazilian
Free-tailed
Bat

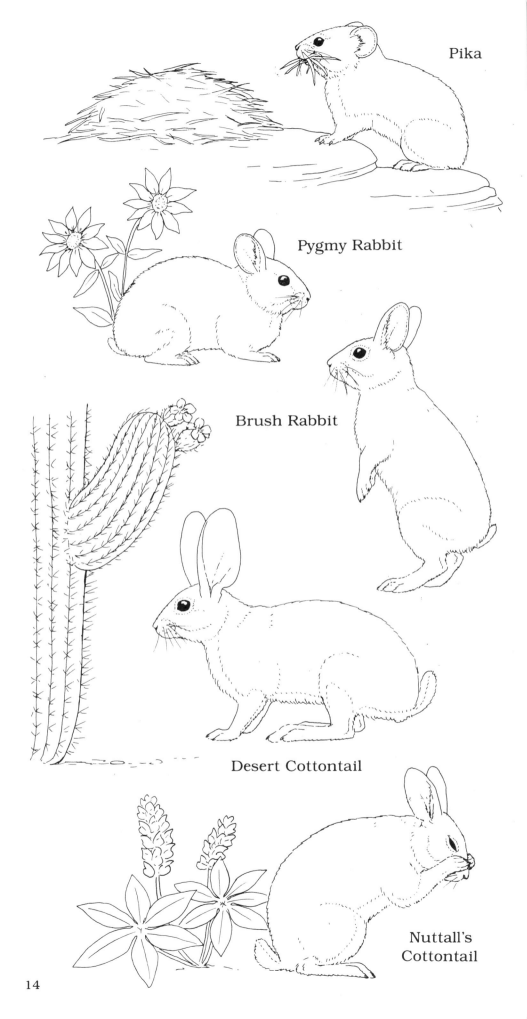

Pika

Pygmy Rabbit

Brush Rabbit

Desert Cottontail

Nuttall's
Cottontail

RABBITS

Although they look like rodents, the rabbits, hares, and pika are in their own order. They have four upper front teeth, whereas rodents have just two. Most members of the rabbit order have long hind legs, short cottony tails, and bulging eyes.

Pika The most unusual member of the rabbit order. Small, with short, rounded ears and no tail. Pikas utter a loud bleat on the open rocky hillsides of our higher western mountains. They dry and store their own hay for the winter. **(25)**

Pygmy Rabbit Our smallest true rabbit. It is slaty pink with small ears and a small gray tail. This rabbit lives in the sagebrush of the Great Basin. **(26)**

Brush Rabbit This rabbit lives in the brush and chaparral of California and Oregon. It is small and dark brown and has small ears and a small tail. **(27)**

Desert Cottontail The common cottontail rabbit of our western valleys. It is pale gray with a yellowish wash and long ears. **(28)**

Nuttall's Cottontail This rabbit replaces the Desert Cottontail in the thickets and rocky areas of our western mountains. It is pale gray, with shorter, black-tipped ears. **(29)**

14

Rabbits (Eastern)

New England Cottontail Inhabits hilly country of our eastern mountains. Slightly redder overall than the Eastern Cottontail, it lacks the rusty nape, but features a black patch between the ears. **(30)**

Eastern Cottontail Widespread east of the Rockies in heavy brush, woods, and fields. This cottontail is grayish brown with a rusty nape and white tops on its feet. It can damage gardens, shrubs, and small trees. **(31)**

Marsh Rabbit Found only near water from Virginia to Florida. It is dark brown with reddish brown tops on its feet. This rabbit searches for bulbs and fresh grass at night and is a good swimmer. **(32)**

Swamp Rabbit Replaces the Marsh Rabbit to the west from Georgia and Illinois to Texas. This long-haired rabbit is somewhat larger and more grayish, with pale rust fur on the top of its feet. It too is a good swimmer. **(33)**

New England Cottontail

Eastern Cottontail

Marsh Rabbit

Swamp Rabbit

15

Snowshoe Hare

summer

winter

European Hare

winter

Arctic Hare

summer

Rabbits: Hares

While rabbits raise and hide their young in nests, hares do not, as their young are born ready to run. Hares and jack-rabbits (which are also hares) have very long ears and can leap up to 20 feet.

Snowshoe Hare Also known as the Varying Hare. Its fur coat varies from all white (with black-tipped ears) in winter to dark brown (including the tail) in summer. Lives in northern forests and does not hibernate. Its wide feet act like snowshoes in winter. **(34)**

European Hare The common hare of Europe and Africa has been introduced to open hill-sides of the Northeast and Ontario. This large hare is brown-ish in summer, grayish in winter. Its tail is always black above. **(35)**

Arctic Hare Resident on the open tundra plains of Canada north of the forest belt. Arctic Hares live in large groups and often stand up on their hind legs. Their coat is gray-brown in summer and white in winter. This hare is replaced by the Alaskan Hare in Alaska. **(36)**

Rabbits: Jackrabbits

These long-eared western hares are able to run at speeds of over 35 mph. Often seen early in the morning or late in the afternoon.

Antelope Jackrabbit This jackrabbit is restricted to cactus forests and desert washes of southern Arizona. Its dark brown back and rump contrast with its bright white sides. The enormous 8-inch ears lack black tips. **(37)**

Black-tailed Jackrabbit Common in prairies and deserts of the Southwest from the Great Plains to California. This jackrabbit is grayish brown with black-tipped ears. The top of the tail and rump are black. **(38)**

White-tailed Jackrabbit More northerly in range, this jackrabbit lives from Wisconsin west to the Cascades. It is brownish gray in summer with a white tail. In winter it becomes white or pale gray, with black-tipped ears. **(39)**

Black-tailed Jackrabbit

Antelope Jackrabbit

White-tailed Jackrabbit

winter

summer

17

Porcupine

Mountain Beaver

Beaver

RODENTS

The commonest and most widespread order of mammals. These mammals have a gap between their two front teeth and the chewing teeth. Rodents are active mainly at night and are chiefly vegetarian.

Porcupine Our only mammal with long sharp quills, which cover all but the belly. Its heavy body looks like a black ball resting in a tree. Porcupines eat bark, buds, and saplings in forested areas of the North and West. **(40)**

Mountain Beaver Not really a beaver, this mammal is usually called by its scientific name: Aplodontia. It looks like a plump Muskrat with no tail. Found only at night in moist forests from California to British Columbia. **(41)**

Beaver Our largest rodent — adults can weigh up to 60 pounds. A Beaver can topple small trees with its huge teeth. This large rodent feeds on bark and twigs. It builds stick and mud dams and lodges on ponds and streams in its home territory. It swims well, using its webbed hind feet. Beavers warn each other of danger by slapping the water with their scaly, paddle-shaped tails. **(42)**

Rodents: Chipmunks

Small, alert, ground-dwelling squirrels that often flick their slightly bushy tails. All chipmunks have erect ears and a set of five dark and four paler stripes on the back. The face is also striped with white. Chipmunks feed on seeds, fruit, and nuts. They build burrows up to 30 feet long with side chambers.

Least Chipmunk Our smallest and most variable chipmunk. Note that its stripes extend to the base of its tail. This chipmunk is found widely in the interior, west from Ontario to the Yukon and south to the Grand Canyon. (43)

Cliff Chipmunk Very pale, with light brown and light gray stripes on the back. Lives in pine and juniper slopes of our southwestern mountains. (44)

Eastern Chipmunk Widespread in wooded areas of the eastern U.S. and Canada. Note the reddish rump. This chipmunk has a bird-like call. It will often come to bird feeders in the suburbs. (45)

Colorado Chipmunk A small chipmunk with red sides and white fur behind the ears. Found in Colorado and bordering states. (46)

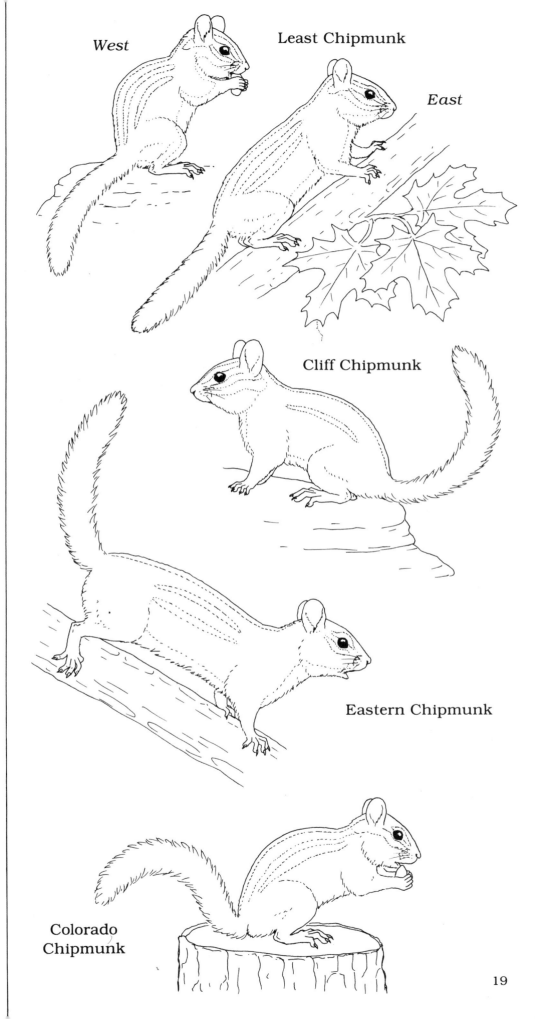

West

Least Chipmunk

East

Cliff Chipmunk

Eastern Chipmunk

Colorado Chipmunk

19

Hoary Marmot

Yellow-bellied Marmot

Woodchuck

Rodents: Marmots

Marmots are giant ground-dwelling squirrels. They have short legs with long digging claws on the front feet. All marmots hibernate during the winter.

Hoary Marmot   Weighing up to 20 pounds, this marmot is silvery gray with a black-and-white head and shoulders. Its shrill whistle rings across rock slides and meadows in mountains from Idaho north through Alaska. (**47**)

Yellow-bellied Marmot   A rich yellowish brown marmot with a yellow belly. Its reddish tail has a black tip. It gives high-pitched chirps from boulders in rocky meadows in our western mountains and valleys. (**48**)

Woodchuck   This is the so-called groundhog that emerges from its winter burrow looking for its shadow. It is uniformly frosted with brown except for the white around the nose. The belly is paler (rusty). The Woodchuck's bushy tail separates it from the Beaver and Muskrat. It is common in fields and woodland edges in the Northeast, Midwest, and across Canada. (**49**)

Rodents: Ground Squirrels

A variable group of small and medium-sized squirrels of central and western America. Many ground squirrels sit up and look like prairie dogs, but a ground squirrel can be recognized by its longer face and tail.

Thirteen-lined Ground Squirrel Attractive, with its dark brown stripes mixed with rows of pale buffy spots. This ground squirrel is common along roadsides and on lawns and golf courses from Ohio west through the Great Plains. **(50)**

Spotted Ground Squirrel This ground squirrel has light buffy spots, like those of the Thirteen-lined Ground Squirrel, but lacks the dark stripes. This pale sandy squirrel matches the color of the soil in the brushlands where it lives in the Southwest. **(51)**

Arctic Ground Squirrel Dusky brown with many tiny pale spots. The legs and feet are tawny. This ground squirrel makes a distinct *sik-sik* call. It is the only ground squirrel living in Alaska and northern Canada. **(52)**

Franklin's Ground Squirrel The largest and darkest ground squirrel of the Midwest and northern Great Plains. It is dark brownish gray with a fairly long tail. **(53)**

Thirteen-lined Ground Squirrel

Arctic Ground Squirrel

Spotted Ground Squirrel

Franklin's Ground Squirrel

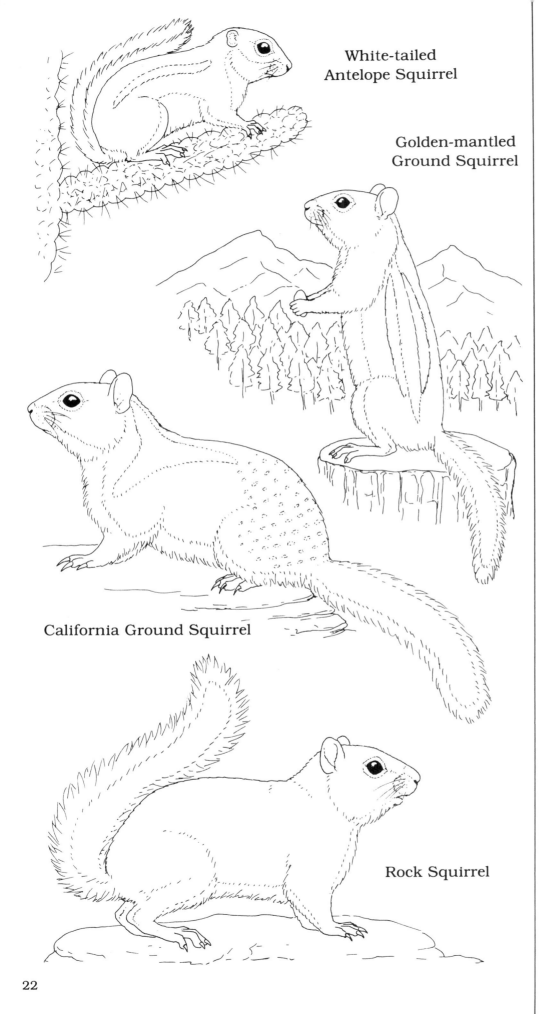

White-tailed
Antelope Squirrel

Golden-mantled
Ground Squirrel

California Ground Squirrel

Rock Squirrel

Rodents: Ground Squirrels

White-tailed Antelope Squirrel Unlike most ground squirrels, this one runs with its tail arched over its back. It has a white stripe on each side of the back. This ground squirrel inhabits deserts of the Southwest and Great Basin. **(54)**

Golden-mantled Ground Squirrel With its striped back, this ground squirrel looks like a giant chipmunk. Note its unstriped reddish head and shoulders. Familiar to campers and tourists in western forests as it begs for hand-outs. **(55)**

California Ground Squirrel Found only in California and western Oregon. This ground squirrel is brown with buffy bands and a gray neck patch. Its white-fringed tail is less bushy than that of a Gray Squirrel. **(56)**

Rock Squirrel A large, mottled gray ground squirrel of rocky areas and canyons of the great Southwest. Some individuals show much black on the head and back. The tail is fairly bushy. **(57)**

Rodents: Prairie Dogs

These rodents have a bark like that of some dogs. Prairie dogs feed on roots, grasses, and flowers on the western Great Plains. These broad-headed squirrels weigh about three pounds and have short, hairy tails. Social animals, they build vast networks of underground burrows and chambers. Once numbering in the billions, they have been poisoned by ranchers and farmers everywhere but in parks and waste areas.

Black-tailed Prairie Dog Our most widespread prairie dog ranges across the shortgrass prairies of the western Great Plains from Montana south to Texas. It has a black-tipped tail. **(58)**

White-tailed Prairie Dog Has a shorter tail than a Blacktail, with a white tip. This prairie dog ranges farther west in Utah, Wyoming, Colorado, Arizona, and New Mexico. It lives in upland meadows and juniper-pine country at elevations from 5000 to 12,000 feet. **(59)**

Black-tailed Prairie Dog

White-tailed
Prairie Dog

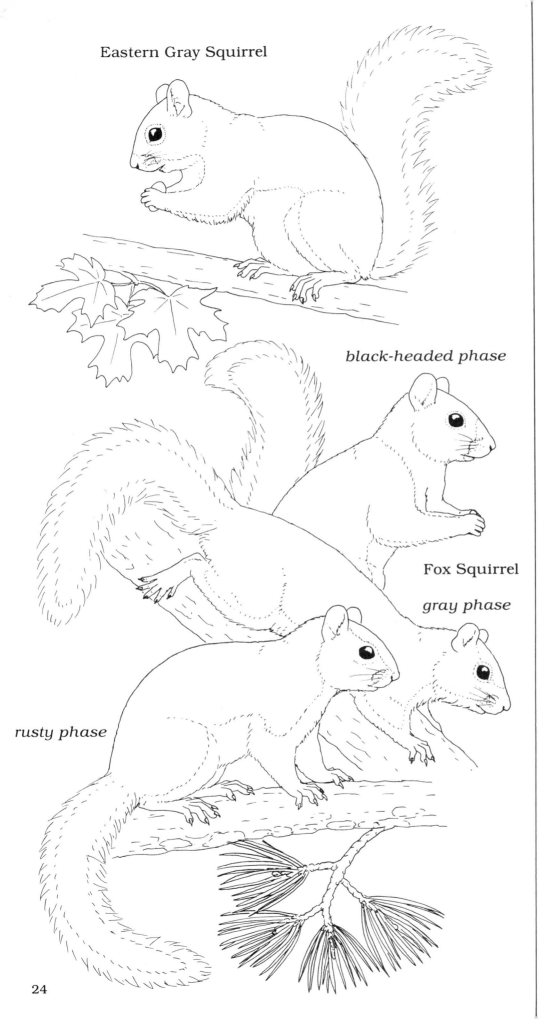

Eastern Gray Squirrel

black-headed phase

Fox Squirrel

gray phase

rusty phase

Rodents: Tree Squirrels (Eastern)

Tree squirrels have longer, bushier tails than ground squirrels do. This helps them keep their balance as they dash about tree limbs.

Eastern Gray Squirrel The most familiar mammal of eastern North America. Abundant in city parks, suburbs, and woodlands. Gray with white underparts, it has a tawny wash in summer. It stores nuts and acorns in the ground, many of which grow into trees. People put out squirrel seed in the winter only to find birds stealing most of it. Black or white individuals are sometimes seen. **(60)**

Fox Squirrel Somewhat larger than a Gray Squirrel, with similar calls and habits. The commonest color phase is rusty yellowish gray with a pale rusty belly. In the area around Chesapeake Bay this squirrel is gray with white around the nose and ears. In the deep South it may be black-headed, with white again around the nose and ears. Widespread east of the Rockies except in the Northeast; found from the Great Lakes and southern Pennsylvania southwards. **(61)**

Rodents: Tree Squirrels (Western)

Western Gray Squirrel   A large gray squirrel with a long, bushy tail and white belly. This squirrel replaces the Eastern Gray Squirrel in the forests of the Pacific Coast. It has blackish feet and lacks the tawny overtones in summer. It thrives in almond and walnut plantations. **(62)**

Tassel-eared Squirrels

These are America's most attractive tree squirrels. As the Colorado River slowly carved the Grand Canyon, two populations of tassel-ears gradually became isolated. These two squirrels now appear very different.

Abert's Squirrel   Found south and east of the Grand Canyon, in ponderosa pines. This squirrel has long, tufted rusty ears; gray sides; a chestnut back; and white underparts. The bushy tail is blackish above, white below. **(63)**

Kaibab Squirrel   Found only on the north rim of Arizona's Grand Canyon, in an area known as the Kaibab Plateau. This squirrel searches for nuts, seeds, and mistletoe in the ponderosa pine country. The tail is all white, and the underparts are black (not white, like an Abert's). **(64)**

Western Gray Squirrel

Abert's Squirrel

Kaibab Squirrel

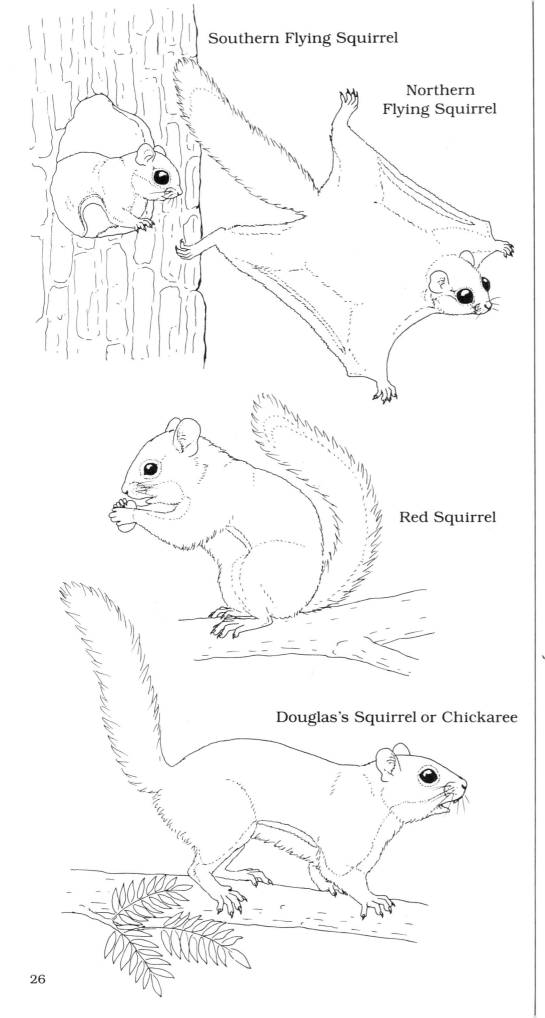

Southern Flying Squirrel

Northern
Flying Squirrel

Red Squirrel

Douglas's Squirrel or Chickaree

Rodents: Flying Squirrels

Small, nocturnal squirrels with large black eyes. Gray-brown to cinnamon above, white below. During the night flying squirrels glide from tree to tree, using the broad folds of skin that connect their front and back feet.

Northern Flying Squirrel This flying squirrel lives in the forests and attics of the northern U.S. and Canada. It is slightly larger than the Southern Flying Squirrel, and the white fur on its underparts is dark at the base. **(65)**

Southern Flying Squirrel This flying squirrel is found from the Gulf of Mexico north to southern Ontario and New England. It is smaller than the Northern, with all-white fur on its belly. **(66)**

Red Squirrels

Two small tree squirrels that are partial to pines and other cone-bearing trees.

Red Squirrel Rusty red with a red tail and a blackish side stripe in summer. In winter this squirrel develops rusty ear tufts, loses the side stripe, and is paler. Common in cooler forests of the Northeast, Rockies, Canada, and Alaska. **(67)**

Douglas's Squirrel (Chickaree) This squirrel replaces the Red Squirrel in the humid forests of the Pacific Northwest. Mostly grayish, it has reddish on its legs and a yellowish belly. The tail is always black. **(68)**

Rodents: Kangaroo Rats

Nighttime rodents of the arid western plains. All kangaroo rats have tiny front feet and long white hind feet. Their powerful thighs are crossed by a white racing stripe. These hopping rodents can jump six feet at a time. The tail is long with a bushy tip. Kangaroo rats feed on seeds and leaves.

Giant Kangaroo Rat At 14 inches long, this is the largest of our 14 species. Its tail tip is dark and it has five toes. This kangaroo rat is found only in inland California. **(69)**

Banner-tailed Kangaroo Rat Found in Arizona, New Mexico, and west Texas. It has a black and white tail with a white tip, and only 4 toes. **(70)**

Plains Pocket Gopher One of a dozen species of pocket gophers that live in the fields of our southern and western states. Pocket gophers have short tails and look like buck-toothed prairie dogs, but a gopher's tail is naked. Pocket gophers are rarely seen except at their burrow entrance. **(71)**

California Pocket Mouse One of 20 small mice with cheek pouches like those of a pocket gopher. Pocket mice look like plain gray kangaroo rats with thin tails. **(72)**

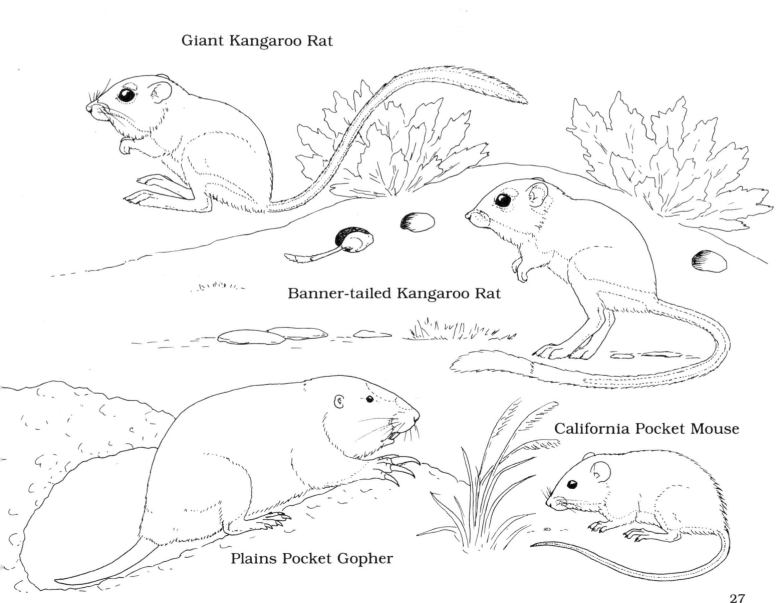

Giant Kangaroo Rat

Banner-tailed Kangaroo Rat

Plains Pocket Gopher

California Pocket Mouse

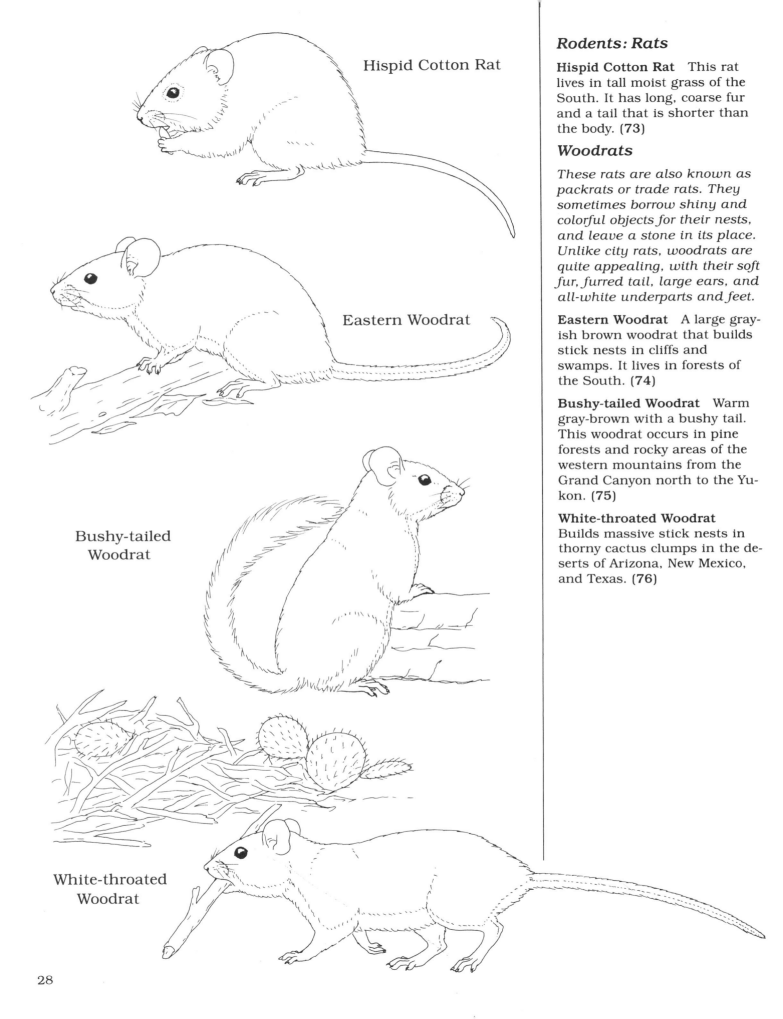

Hispid Cotton Rat

Eastern Woodrat

Bushy-tailed
Woodrat

White-throated
Woodrat

Rodents: Rats

Hispid Cotton Rat This rat lives in tall moist grass of the South. It has long, coarse fur and a tail that is shorter than the body. (**73**)

Woodrats

These rats are also known as packrats or trade rats. They sometimes borrow shiny and colorful objects for their nests, and leave a stone in its place. Unlike city rats, woodrats are quite appealing, with their soft fur, furred tail, large ears, and all-white underparts and feet.

Eastern Woodrat A large grayish brown woodrat that builds stick nests in cliffs and swamps. It lives in forests of the South. (**74**)

Bushy-tailed Woodrat Warm gray-brown with a bushy tail. This woodrat occurs in pine forests and rocky areas of the western mountains from the Grand Canyon north to the Yukon. (**75**)

White-throated Woodrat Builds massive stick nests in thorny cactus clumps in the deserts of Arizona, New Mexico, and Texas. (**76**)

Rodents: Native Mice

White-footed Mouse   A large-eared mouse, rich reddish brown above, with contrasting pure white feet and underparts. (Adults are reddish brown; the young are gray.) This mouse makes nests in old bird nests and sheds. It is active all year in forests from New England west to Arizona and Montana. **(77)**

Golden Mouse   A very pretty golden cinnamon mouse of trees, vines, and brush of the Southeast. It feeds on insects and seeds of poison ivy and sumac. **(78)**

Pinyon Mouse   A western mouse that lives in rocky terrain with scattered pines. It has a bicolored tail (darker above) and enormous ears. **(79)**

Woodland Jumping Mouse   A very long-tailed mouse with large hind feet. It hops about forests of the Northeast and the Great Lakes region at night. This jumping mouse has a brown back, bright yellowish sides, and a white belly. **(80)**

Southern Grasshopper Mouse   Most rodents eat seeds and plants, but this mouse eats beetles, other mice, grasshoppers, scorpions, and lizards. It occasionally eats a few seeds. Its coat can be grayish or a pinkish cinnamon color. The belly is white, and the short tail is largely white. This mouse hunts at night in the deserts of the Southwest. **(81)**

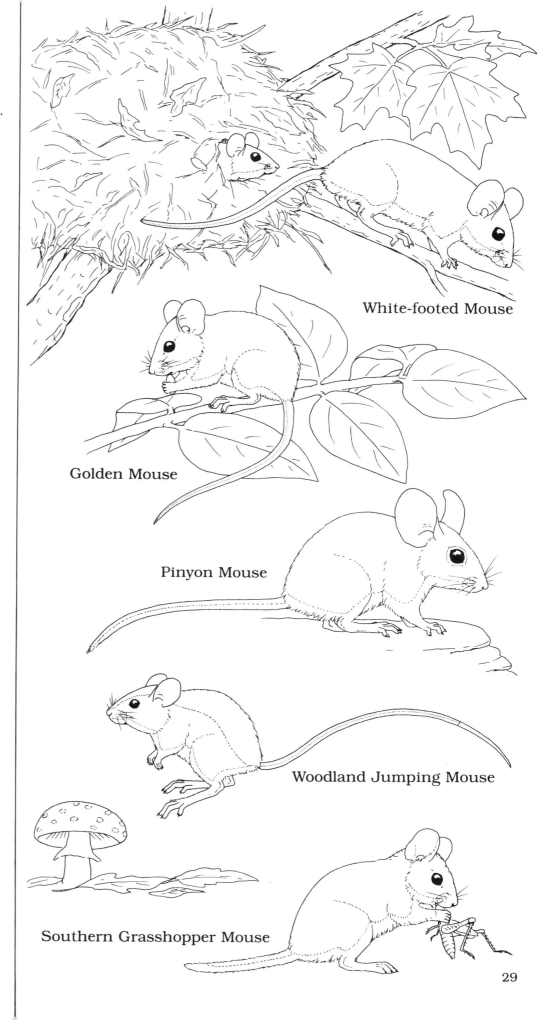

White-footed Mouse

Golden Mouse

Pinyon Mouse

Woodland Jumping Mouse

Southern Grasshopper Mouse

Red Tree Vole

Southern Red-backed Vole

Meadow Vole

Woodland Vole

Collared Lemming

Rodents: Voles

Voles differ from mice by their small ears and short tails. These seed-eaters are active day and night.

Red Tree Vole Unlike other voles, this vole lives high in the spruce, hemlock, and fir forests of northern California and western Oregon. It builds huge twig nests up to 150 feet above ground. This vole is bright red. **(82)**

Southern Red-backed Vole This vole has a reddish back that contrasts with its grayish sides. It inhabits cool moist forests of Canada and the northern U.S. **(83)**

Meadow Vole This vole is widespread in meadows and brush near water. It is dark brown in the East and more grayish brown in the West. **(84)**

Woodland Vole Formerly called the Pine Vole, the Woodland Vole lives in the broadleaf forests of the eastern and southern U.S. It is auburn-colored and has tiny ears and a very short tail. **(85)**

Collared Lemming Lemmings are chunky, short-tailed residents of the arctic tundra of Canada and Alaska. This lemming is all white in winter. In summer it has a mottled gray-brown coat with rusty underparts, a pale face, and a black back stripe. Like other lemmings, it is common some years and very rare in others. **(86)**

Aquatic Rodents

Round-tailed Muskrat This water rat of Florida and the Okefenokee builds woven sedge nests at the base of stumps. It feeds on water plants and crayfish. The tail is round, not flattened as in northern Muskrats. **(87)**

Muskrat A widespread furbearer of marshes, lakes, and streams. The Muskrat has rich brown fur and a long, scaly tail that is flattened from side to side. This large rodent marks its territory with a musky odor. Muskrats feed on cattails, sedges, lilies, frogs, and clams. They build large rounded houses made from cattails, mud, and roots. **(88)**

Nutria A giant South American relative of the Muskrat that can weigh up to 25 pounds. It is grayer and has a longer tail that is round, not flattened as in a Muskrat. Nutria that have escaped from fur farms are living and breeding in the wild in the South and Pacific Northwest. New populations are showing up elsewhere in the U.S. **(89)**

Round-tailed Muskrat

Muskrat

Nutria

31

House Mouse

Brown Rat
or Norway Rat

Black Rat
or Ship Rat

Old World Rodents

Invaders from Asia and Europe, these rodents have become serious pests. They can be told from our native mice and rats by their long, naked tails. These mice and rats are great nuisances and carriers of disease. They live in our streets, buildings, and dumps.

House Mouse A small, all-gray mouse lacking the white underparts of our native mice. Its scaly tail is about as long as its body. The House Mouse lives in houses and barns everywhere. **(90)**

Brown Rat Also known as the Norway, Sewer, or House Rat. It adapted to man in Asia, spread into Europe in the 1500s, and emigrated to the New World around 1776. This rat is gray-brown all over. Its gray tail is shorter than its body. The Brown Rat digs its own tunnels and forces the Black Rat to leave its territory. **(91)**

Black Rat Also known as the Ship or Roof Rat, this rat is less aggressive than the Brown Rat. The Brown Rat now controls the streets. The Black Rat gradually invaded Europe from Asia long before the Brown Rat, and came to North America in the early 1600s. This rat's coat can be black or brown, but its tail is always longer than its body. **(92)**

WHALES

Despite their fish-like form, whales are air-breathing mammals, unlike sharks or other fishes. Dolphins and porpoises are small whales. Seals and manatees are marine (sea-dwelling) mammals, but are not closely related to whales and dolphins.

All whales have two front flippers and a flat tail. They breathe through 1 or 2 nostrils (the blowhole) at the top of the head. Most whales are fast swimmers and deep divers. Fortunately, most nations no longer allow the killing of these majestic citizens of the oceans.

Beluga Also known as the White Whale, the Beluga is a small whale of cold arctic waters from Alaska around Canada to the Maritimes. Note its high forehead, short snout, and the lack of a fin on its back. The young are brown, turning white at six years of age. **(93)**

Narwhal Another denizen of cold arctic seas from Alaska to Greenland. Both males and females are patchy brown in color. Narwhals have no snout and no fin on the back. They have only two upper front teeth. In males the left one grows into a long, hollow, twisted tusk up to 9 feet long. **(94)**

Beluga
or White Whale

Narwhal

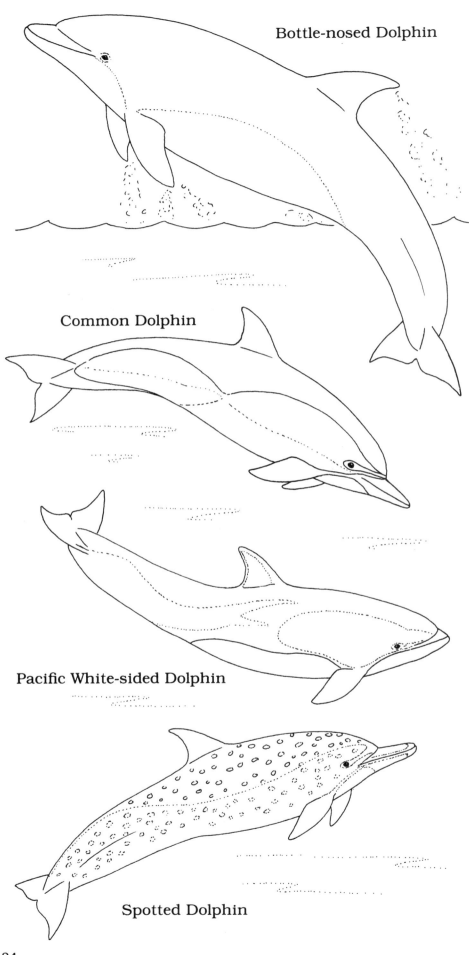

Bottle-nosed Dolphin

Common Dolphin

Pacific White-sided Dolphin

Spotted Dolphin

Whales: Dolphins

These small whales have a large fin on the back and notched tail flukes. Dolphins often travel in large groups, frequently clearing the surface in a series of leaps. They also ride bow waves of ships.

Bottle-nosed Dolphin Large and all grayish, with a whiter belly. Off California this dolphin has white on the upper lip. The Atlantic Coast populations have no white there. **(95)**

Common Dolphin This dolphin is found off both coasts. It is black above, with black flippers, yellow flanks, and a white belly. There are black "spectacles" behind the long beak. **(96)**

Pacific White-sided Dolphin A blunt-nosed, greenish black dolphin with whitish sides and belly. Related species are found along both coasts. **(97)**

Spotted Dolphin A blackish dolphin with large white spots; it is paler below. This dolphin is fairly common in the Gulf of Mexico and northward to the Carolinas. **(98)**

Whales: Dolphins

Pilot Whale   This whale travels in large schools in the Atlantic north of Virginia. Also known as Blackfish, it is an all-black dolphin with a bulging forehead and a large, swept-back fin on its back. (**99**)

Grampus   A large dolphin with a bulging yellowish head and no beak. The flippers are gray and slender. The Grampus is found off both coasts. Males are blue-gray above, females brownish. (**100**)

Harbor Porpoise   A small dolphin with a triangular back fin. The Harbor Porpoise is common close to shore in cooler waters off both coasts. Note its round mouth, black back, pink sides, and white belly. (**101**)

Dall's Porpoise   All black with a striking white area on the sides and belly. This dolphin is found only from California to Alaska. (**102**)

Killer Whale   A huge dolphin, often called Orca. It is black with white on belly and sides. The best marks are the long, pointed dorsal fin and the white spot behind the eye. Killer Whales prey on fish and sea mammals off both coasts. (**103**)

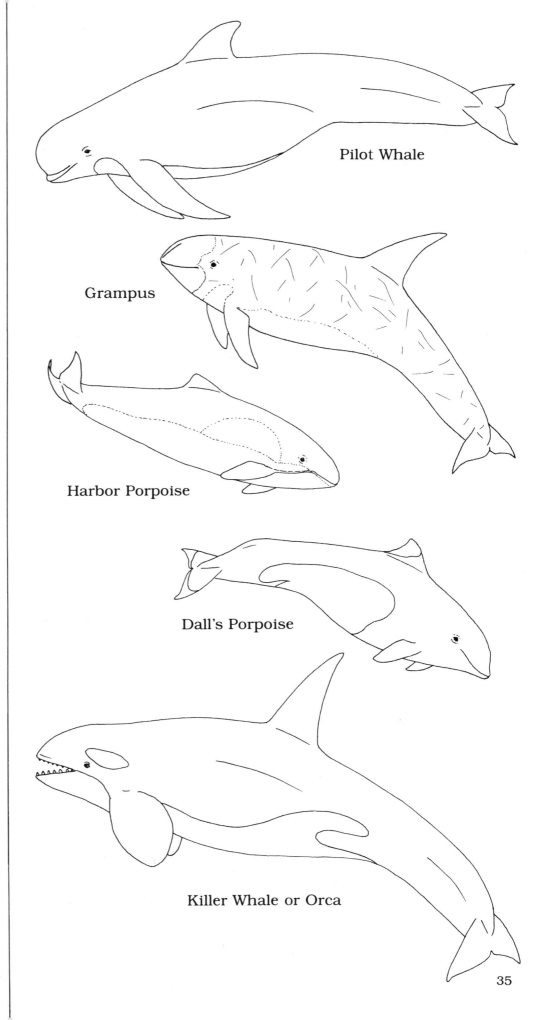

Pilot Whale

Grampus

Harbor Porpoise

Dall's Porpoise

Killer Whale or Orca

Whales

The Sperm Whale has large teeth, but most other large whales have long, comb-like strips of baleen (whalebone) hanging from the upper jaw. This baleen strains tiny shrimp and fish from the rich ocean water.

Hump-backed Whale   A black whale with white undersides and very long white flippers that have knobs on the leading edge. The pointed head is adorned with fleshy knobs. This whale is known for its lovely underwater songs and its spectacular breaching above the water. **(104)**

Right Whale   This whale was considered the "right" whale to harpoon, as it floated instead of sinking after it was killed. It is a huge, heavy-headed, black whale with no fin on its back. Its head often has large raised knobs. The Right Whale is rare but present off both coasts. It migrates north and south with the seasons. **(105)**

Bowhead Whale   Similar to the Right Whale, replacing it in cold arctic seas. The Bowhead is named for its bowed, white lower jaw. Its head makes up almost half of its length. **(106)**

Gray Whale   A medium-sized, blotchy gray whale with no dorsal fin. This whale feeds close to shore among rocks and kelp. The females calve in the lagoons of Baja California. Gray Whales migrate along the Pacific Coast to Alaska for the summers. **(107)**

Sperm Whale
(with Giant Squid)

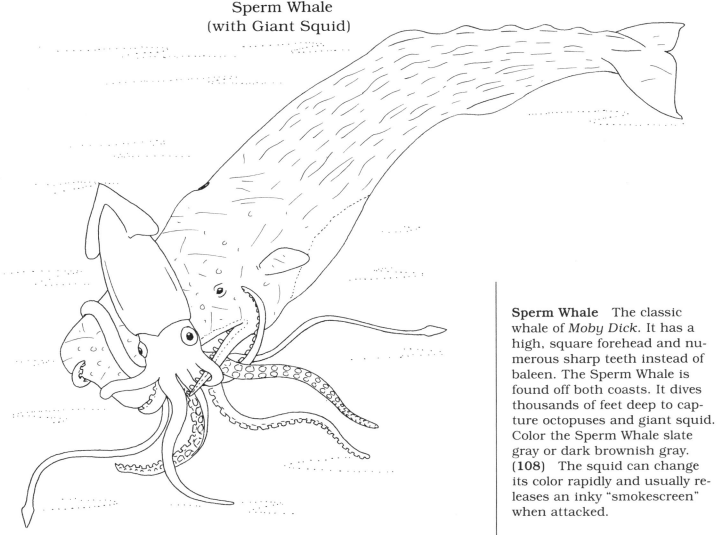

Sperm Whale   The classic whale of *Moby Dick*. It has a high, square forehead and numerous sharp teeth instead of baleen. The Sperm Whale is found off both coasts. It dives thousands of feet deep to capture octopuses and giant squid. Color the Sperm Whale slate gray or dark brownish gray. **(108)**   The squid can change its color rapidly and usually releases an inky "smokescreen" when attacked.

36

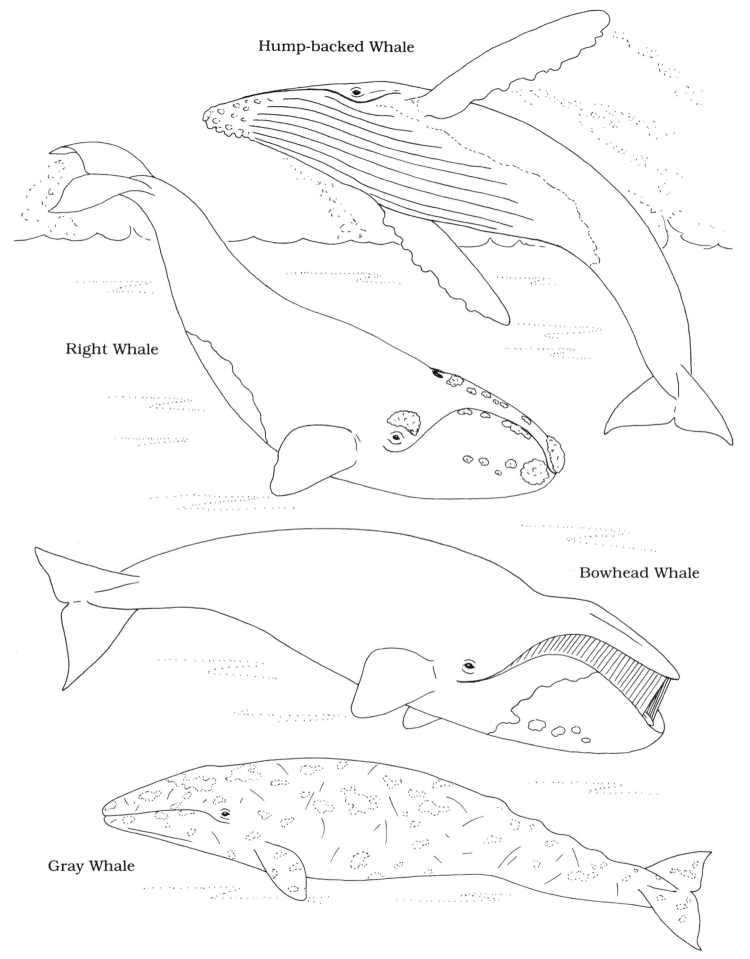

Hump-backed Whale

Right Whale

Bowhead Whale

Gray Whale

37

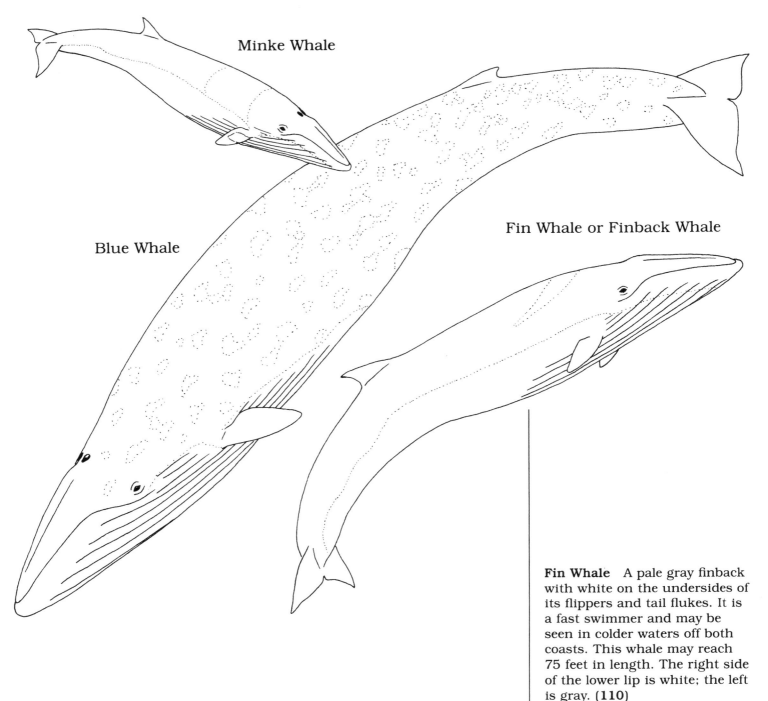

Minke Whale

Blue Whale

Fin Whale or Finback Whale

Whales: Finbacks

All finbacks have baleen instead of teeth, a small fin on the back, and many grooves on the throat. These whales are found off both coasts.

Minke Whale The smallest finback, up to 30 feet long. Blue-gray above and white below, with a distinctive white patch on its flippers. This small whale will approach boats. At close range its white baleen may be noted. **(109)** The **Sei Whale** (not shown) is larger than a Minke — it reaches 50 feet. It has no white on its long flippers and its tail flukes are all dark. Its baleen is black.

Fin Whale A pale gray finback with white on the undersides of its flippers and tail flukes. It is a fast swimmer and may be seen in colder waters off both coasts. This whale may reach 75 feet in length. The right side of the lower lip is white; the left is gray. **(110)**

Blue Whale Weighing up to 200 tons and reaching 100 feet in length, this whale is the largest animal ever to have lived — larger than any dinosaur. This huge whale is blue-gray above with a yellowish belly. It has a tiny fin on its back. The few survivors from commercial whaling eat tiny shrimp called krill. Like other baleen whales, Blue Whales gulp huge mouthfuls of sea water and strain their food from it by using their baleen as a sieve. The baleen of this whale is black. **(111)**

CARNIVORES

This order includes the dogs, cats, bears, raccoons, and weasels. All carnivores have long canine teeth. Carnivores are meat-eaters that capture other animals for food, although most eat some plant food at times. North America has both the largest and smallest carnivores in the world.

Dogs

The wolves, foxes, and coyotes have a long muzzle, erect triangular ears, long legs, and a bushy tail. Their senses of smell, sight, and hearing are acute. Unlike cats, dogs are unable to retract their claws.

Red Wolf A southern wolf with reddish legs, muzzle, and ears. Smaller and less powerful than the Gray Wolf. Both the Red and Gray wolves run with the tail held high. Nearly extinct, this wolf needs strong support for reintroduction attempts. It formerly ranged north to Pennsylvania and west to Texas. **(112)**

Gray Wolf Our largest wild dog — males weigh up to 120 pounds. Most Gray Wolves are grizzled gray; a few are white or black, but all have a black-tipped tail (unlike a Red Fox). Gray Wolves run in packs of up to a dozen, with a dominant male and many females, including both mothers and other females that help take care of the young. Gray Wolves talk to each other by means of a wide variety of howls and barks. They run with the tail held high (unlike a Coyote). The Gray Wolf has been killed off everywhere except for the western Great Lakes region, Canada, and Alaska. **(113)**

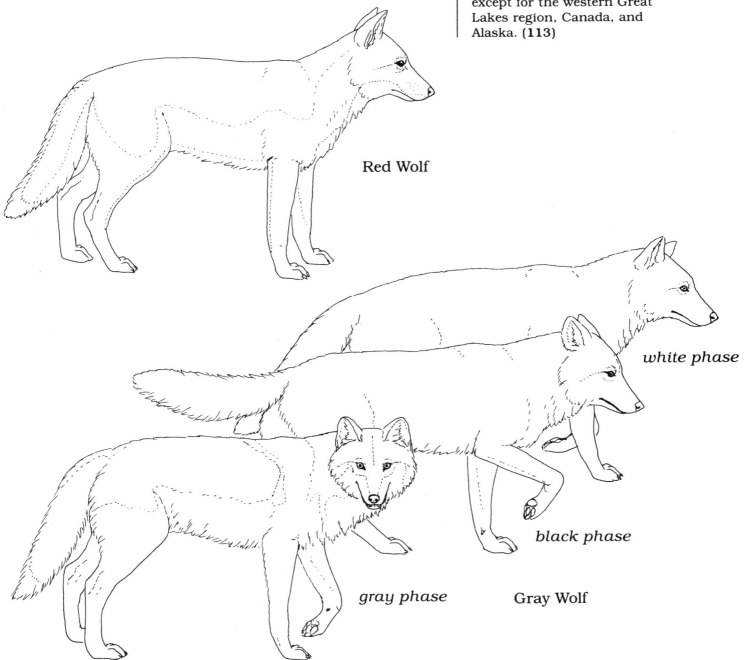

Red Wolf

white phase

black phase

gray phase

Gray Wolf

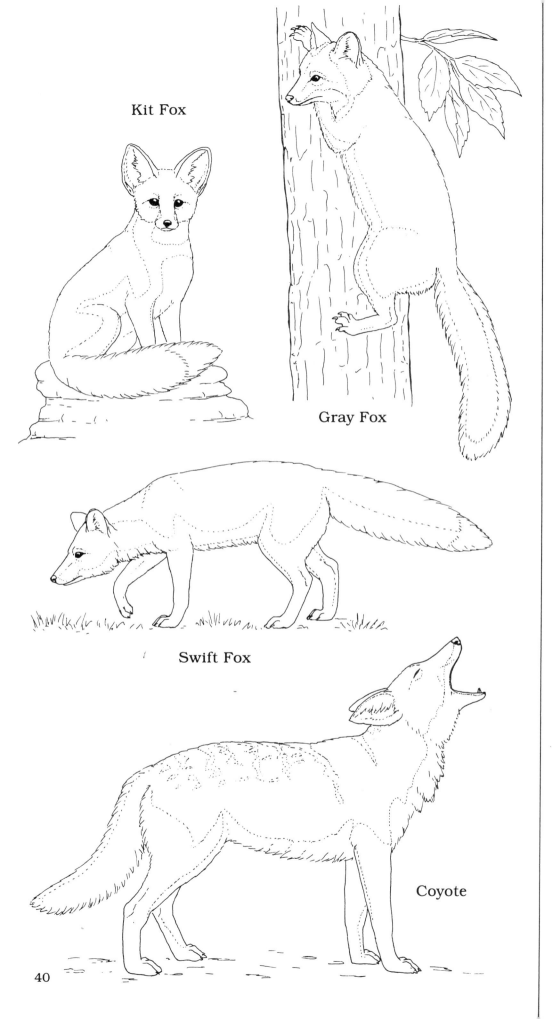

Kit Fox

Gray Fox

Swift Fox

Coyote

Carnivores: Dogs

Gray Fox   This fox has a pepper-and-salt gray coat, with rusty patches on the neck, belly, legs, and tail. The black muzzle contrasts with the white cheeks and throat. The tail is black-tipped, not white. This fox climbs trees, rocks, and scrub, searching for rodents and fruit. (**114**)

Kit Fox   A small, pale gray fox with large ears and a black tail tip. This fox hunts rodents at night in deserts of the Southwest. (**115**)

Swift Fox   A small buffy yellow fox with large ears and a black spot on each side of the snout. It too has a black tail tip. The Swift Fox hunts rodents and insects on the Great Plains from Texas to Canada. (**116**)

Coyote   Catches roadrunners, lizards, snakes, rodents, and rabbits in chases at speeds up to 40 mph. A Coyote is larger than a fox and smaller than a wolf. It poses no danger to man, but has been ruthlessly killed as a threat to livestock. Coyotes vary from gray to reddish. They are usually seen by day and heard by night. Coyotes are occasionally seen in suburbs in the West and have spread eastward to the wilder parts of Massachusetts. (**117**)

Carnivores: Dogs

Arctic Fox Found only beyond treeline in northern Canada and Alaska. In summer all are brownish slate in color with no white on the tail. In winter most Arctic Foxes turn all white. In coastal southwestern Alaska this fox is brownish slate year 'round. The Arctic Fox chases rodents and birds, eats berries, and follows Polar Bears so it can feed on their leftovers. **(118)**

Red Fox The classic quarry of the fox hunter on horseback, and a pack of yelping hounds. This fox is typically reddish yellow with black legs and a white tail tip. A black phase occurs as well as a cross phase that has gray fur and a blackish back. This fox is chiefly active at night, searching for rodents, insects, birds, and berries. The Red Fox occurs widely in northern and eastern states and provinces. It weighs up to 15 pounds. **(119)**

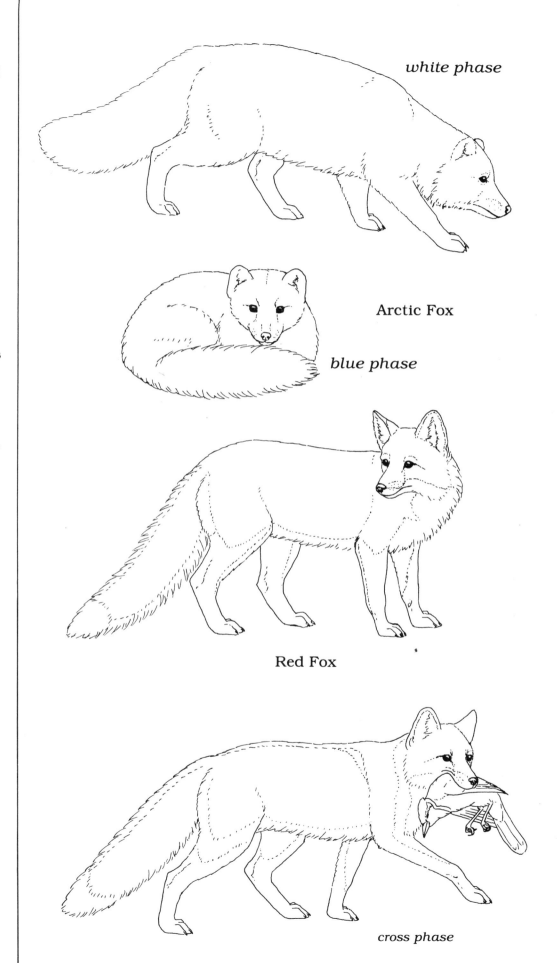

white phase

Arctic Fox

blue phase

Red Fox

cross phase

41

Black Bear

black phase

cinnamon phase

Polar Bear

Carnivores: Bears

The world's largest land-dwelling carnivores. Bears walk on the entire foot, rather than on the toes as cats and dogs do. Bears have tiny tails, small ears, and small eyes. Their eyesight is poor, but their sense of smell is superb. Most bears spend much of the winter in a den.

Black Bear   Our smallest bear is black in the East, but occasionally cinnamon or even blue-gray in the West. Its face is always brown, and it often has a white patch on the chest. This bear will forage by day, particularly in national parks. Its face is roundish. The Black Bear roams forests, swamps, and mountains, searching for berries, nuts, insects, birds, small mammals, honey, and garbage. **(120)**

Polar Bear   A black-nosed, very large white bear, often with a yellowish tinge. Polar Bears are excellent swimmers and weigh between 600 and 1100 pounds. Polar Bears stalk birds, seals, and other mammals on ice floes and arctic tundra in northern Alaska and Canada. This bear is very dangerous to approach. **(121)**

Carnivores: Bears

Grizzly Bear White tips on its yellow and brown hair give this bear a grizzled appearance. Its face is dish-shaped, and it has a big hump at the shoulder. It digs up rodents with its long front claws. A Grizzly makes its own trails as it searches for small mammals, birds, berries, and fish. Once widespread in the West, it survives chiefly in national parks such as Yellowstone, Glacier, Banff, Jasper, and Denali. It can weigh up to 850 pounds. Avoid it. **(122)**

"Kodiak Bear" A huge subspecies of Grizzly Bear, found only on Kodiak and neighboring islands in Gulf of Alaska. **(123)**

"Alaska Brown Bear" Another huge Alaskan Grizzly, averaging nine feet long. This Grizzly lives along the forested coast of southern Alaska. It is dark brown with a yellowish tinge. This bear emerges from its den in spring to feed on seaweed and winter-killed animals. It grazes on grasses and sedges, catches rodents, and congregates at salmon runs. Unprovoked attacks on humans are rare. **(124)**

Grizzly Bear

Kodiak Bear

Alaska Brown Bear

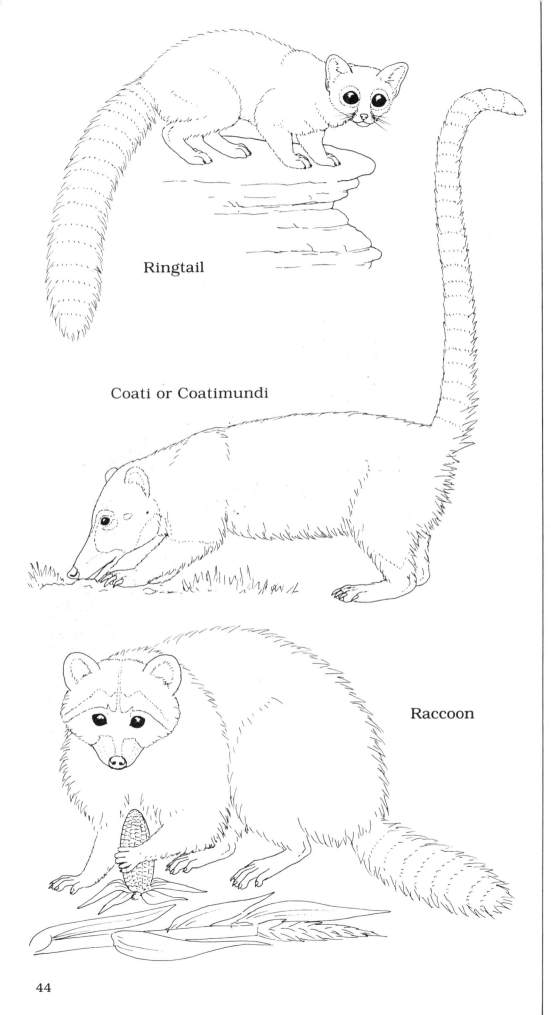

Ringtail

Coati or Coatimundi

Raccoon

Carnivores: Raccoons

Dog-sized mammals with longish tails that feature rings or bands. These mammals live in small family groups and eat a wide variety of animal and vegetable foods.

Ringtail Formerly called the Ring-tailed Cat. Cat-like in motion, it pursues mice, birds, insects, and lizards. The Ringtail hunts at night in woods, brush, caves, and rocky areas of the West. It is pale yellowish gray, with short legs and a long, ringed tail. **(125)**

Coati Also known as the Coatimundi. It has a long snout and a long, faintly banded tail, which is often carried high. The Coati is active in bands by day in forested hills and canyons of Arizona, New Mexico, and west Texas. **(126)**

Raccoon The well-known masked "bandit" that raids garbage cans. The Raccoon lives in woods and by streams, and is now moving into cities. Its coat is brownish gray and the tail has rings of black and yellowish white. It searches by day or night for fruits, nuts, insects, frogs, and fish. **(127)**

Carnivores: Weasels

A diverse family that includes weasels, badgers, skunks, otters, and minks. They are small to medium in size, with low bodies, a longish tail, and short ears. Many use scent glands to protect food caches or for defense.

Marten About the size of a Mink, but with yellowish brown fur and a bushy tail. Its legs and tail are dark brown, while its throat and breast are pale buffy. The Marten chases squirrels through the northern forests. It usually hunts in dim light and by night. It also hunts for rabbits, mice, birds, and berries. **(128)**

Fisher Weighing up to 12 pounds, a Fisher is much larger than a Mink or Marten. It is dark brownish black with white-tipped hairs that give it a frosted look. Resident in northern forests, it is active night and day, searching for snowshoe hares, squirrels, mice, and porcupines. It does not fish. **(129)**

Mink Widespread in much of the U.S. and Canada, the Mink is dark brown with a white chin patch. It has a smaller tail than a Marten or Fisher. It hunts fish, crayfish, frogs, birds, and small mammals along shores and while swimming. **(130)**

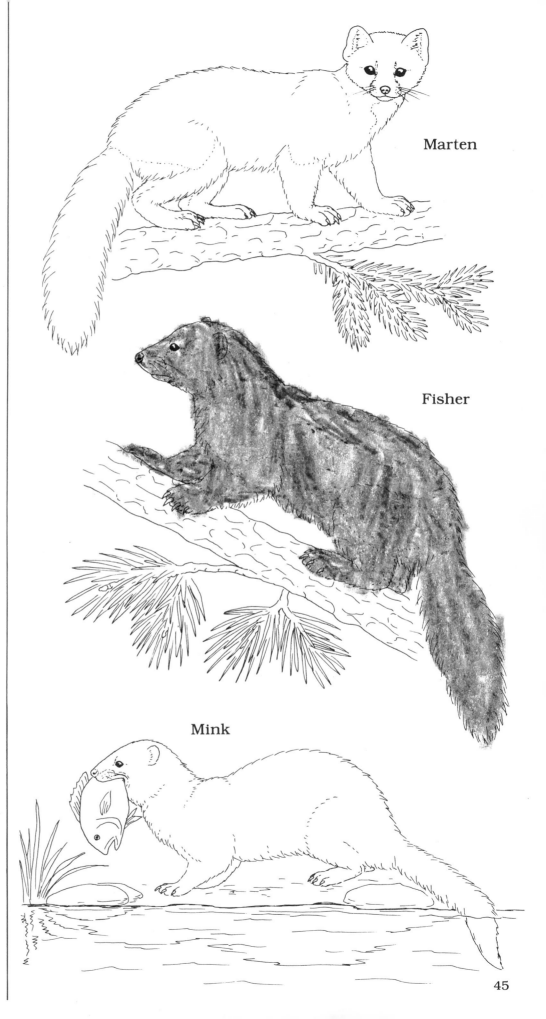

Marten

Fisher

Mink

45

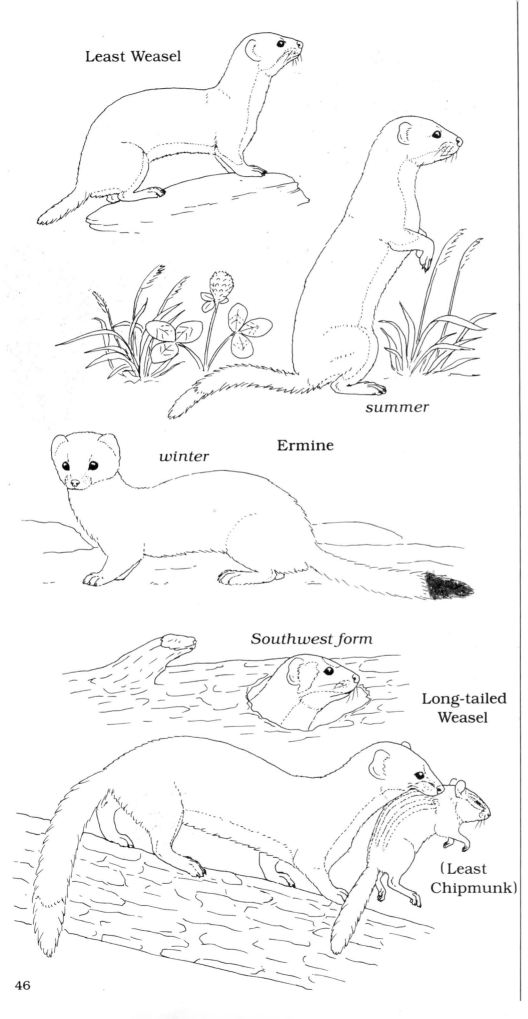

Least Weasel

summer

winter   Ermine

Southwest form

Long-tailed
Weasel

(Least
Chipmunk)

Carnivores: Weasels

Least Weasel The smallest carnivore in the world. It is all brown above and white below with white feet. This weasel has a very short tail, which is brown in summer and all white in winter. The Least Weasel is found between the Rockies and the Appalachians. In the North it becomes all white in winter. **(131)**

Ermine Also called the Short-tailed Weasel. In the warmer months it is dark brown above with white feet and a black tail tip. The white winter coat retains the black tail tip. This expert mouser lives in bushy and wooded areas from Virginia to Alaska. **(132)**

Long-tailed Weasel Occurs in 48 states and southernmost Canada; the only weasel found in the Sun Belt. It has a long, black-tipped tail; yellowish white underparts; and dark brown feet. Northern individuals become white in winter, except for a black tail tip. In the Southwest, a form with white patches on its face occurs. **(133)**

Carnivores: Weasels

Wolverine The largest weasel, weighing up to 60 pounds. The Wolverine looks like a small bear with a heavy, bushy tail and a yellowish forehead. The dark brown body sports broad yellow racing stripes on each side, extending from the shoulders to the base of the tail. Wolverines hunt beavers, deer, porcupines, and birds in remote forests and tundra from the Rockies to Alaska. **(134)**

Black-footed Ferret America's most endangered mammal. This weasel was formerly widespread in the vast colonies of its prey, the prairie dogs. As ranchers and farmers poisoned most dogtowns, the Black-footed Ferret became nearly extinct. Today only a few dozen are left. The Ferret is buffy with black feet and tail tip. Its face is white with a black "bandit" mask. **(135)**

Badger Note the black-and-white face, and the white stripe from the nose over the shoulders. The Badger's body is gray with a yellowish tail and belly. It has long front claws used in digging for rodents. Its long hair protects it from rattlesnake bites. **(136)**

Wolverine

Black-footed Ferret

Badger

Spotted Skunk

Striped Skunk.

Hooded Skunk

Hog-nosed Skunk

Carnivores: Skunks

Skunks are black with various white patterns. Their long fluffy tails are often held over their backs. When threatened they can spray a foul-smelling liquid up to 15 feet. Avoid them. Skunks eat a variety of plants and animals.

Spotted Skunk   Our smallest skunk, with a patchwork of spots and stripes. It lives in trees, brush, and open areas west of the Mississippi and south of the Ohio River. **(137)**

Striped Skunk   Occurs in 48 states and southern Canada. This common skunk is primarily active at night. Its presence can be noted along roads in the woods, prairies, and suburbs. It has a white nape and two broad white stripes on each side. **(138)**

Hooded Skunk   This skunk features a shaggy neck and a very long black tail. Its pattern varies widely, with differing amounts of white on the back and sides. When it has white side stripes, they are usually thin. It is found along streams and brushy hillsides in Arizona, New Mexico, and south Texas. **(139)**

Hog-nosed Skunk   The long, pig-like snout and oversized front claws of this skunk help it dig up plant tubers, insects, and snakes. It is found only in Texas, New Mexico, and Arizona. **(140)**

Carnivores: Otters

These large aquatic weasels should not be confused with seals, which lack tails.

River Otter   Rich brown fur, with a silvery sheen below. Adapted for swimming, with its webbed feet and long, thick tail. This social, playful mammal swims rapidly under or at the water surface. Look for its slides worn into streambanks and snowbanks. River Otters feed on fish, frogs, and other aquatic animals. Too many have been lost to trappers and pollution. (**141**)

Sea Otter   A delightful ocean-dwelling otter that lives along Pacific shores from California to Alaska. It is dark brown, with a yellowish gray face and neck. The Sea Otter holds captured sea urchins and shellfish on its chest and bangs them open with a rock tool while floating on its back. It sleeps at sea, coming ashore only during storms. Conservationists saved it from near extinction in the early 1900s. (**142**)

River Otter

Sea Otter

49

Carnivores: Cats

Unlike dogs, cats can spread out or withdraw their claws. Cats also tend to have shorter faces and smaller ears than dogs. Most cats have superb eyesight and hunt at night. The wild cats have thin tails that are never bushy.

Jaguar This powerful Latin American cat once ranged widely from Texas to California. Its tawny coat is covered with rosettes of black spots, some with spots in the center. The Jaguar used to hunt peccaries, rodents, birds, and stray cattle, but it has not been seen north of the border in years. It can weigh up to 250 pounds. **(143)**

Mountain Lion Also known as Puma or Cougar, our lion is large and long, with a yellowish brown or gray coat. Its long tail is tipped with dark brown. The backs of the ears and sides of the face are also dark brown. Adults are unspotted; young are spotted. This large cat hunts deer, hares, rodents, and raccoons in wild forests, scrubland, and mountains, chiefly in the West. **(144)**

Jaguar

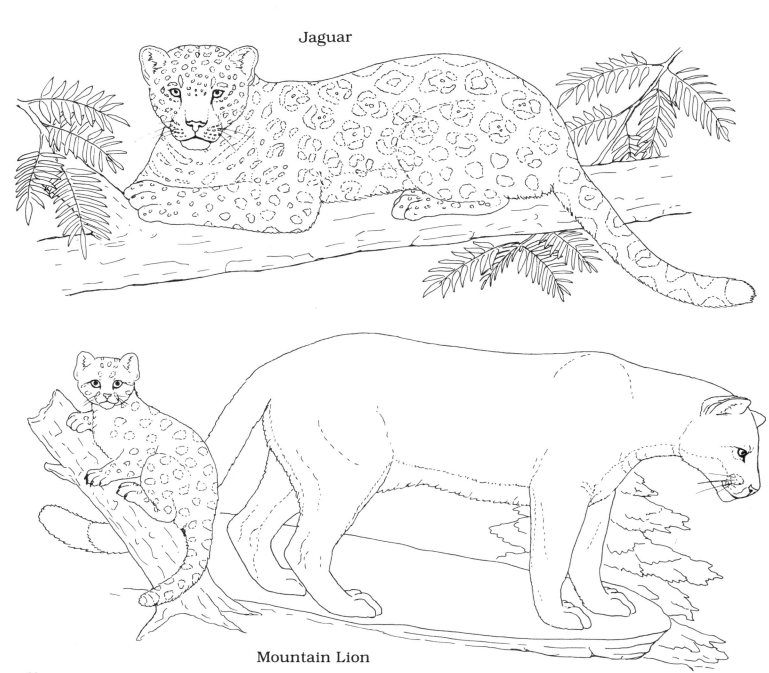

Mountain Lion

Carnivores: Cats

Margay A rare resident of southern Texas, the Margay looks like a small Ocelot with a longer tail. It is buffy with a pattern of brown stripes and spots. This cat lives in woodland, and weighs only up to 7 pounds. **(145)**

Ocelot Larger than a Margay, weighing up to 40 pounds. It has rows of blackish spots, making it appear striped. The tail is much longer than that of a Bobcat. The Ocelot hunts at night in thick thornscrub of southern Texas and Arizona. It is rare, and is now protected in the U.S. **(146)**

Jaguarundi A rare unspotted cat with very short legs and a long thin tail. About the size of a house cat. It has two color phases: all gray or all reddish. Hunts rodents, rabbits, and birds in scrub and streams of southern Texas and Arizona. **(147)**

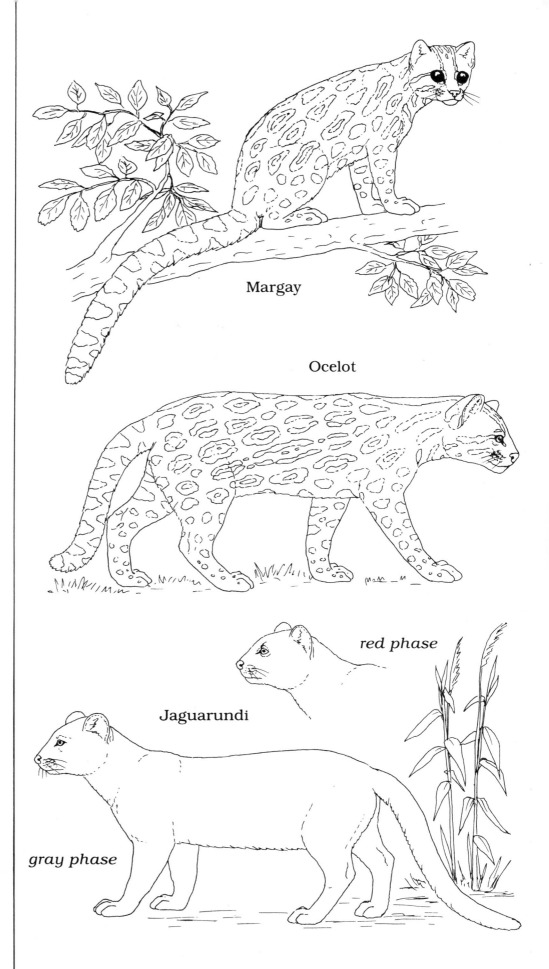

Margay

Ocelot

red phase

Jaguarundi

gray phase

Lynx

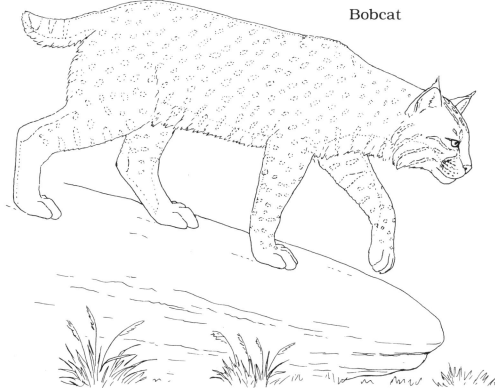

Bobcat

Carnivores: Cats

Lynx   The bob-tailed cat of the northern woods. The Lynx has long ear tufts, a facial ruff, and a black tail tip. Its huge wide paws help it walk over snow as it chases Snowshoe Hares, rodents, and birds. It weighs up to 30 pounds and sports long, soft, grayish buff fur, which is mottled with brown. It is rarely seen but widespread in forests of Alaska, Canada, and the northern U.S. (**148**)

Bobcat   A southern cousin of the Lynx, often called the "wildcat." Found widely from Canada to Mexico in wild country, it is now absent from much of the Midwest. Its coat is warm reddish brown in summer and much grayer in winter, with many small dark spots (particularly on the legs). Known for its wild screams, the Bobcat hunts birds and mammals at night in woods, swamps, and rocky country. (**149**)

SEALS

Seals are ocean-dwelling mammals that feed mostly on fish. Their torpedo-like bodies have front and hind flippers, but no visible tail. Their fur appears dark when wet, pale when dry. Seals haul out onto rocks, beaches, and sea ice to rest and raise young.

Eared Seals

These seals with small external ears can turn their hind flippers forward to aid in "walking." The male fur seals and sea lions are up to 4 times larger than the females.

Northern Fur Seal This fur seal breeds chiefly on the Pribilof Islands west of Alaska and winters at sea, south to California. The 600-pound males are blackish with a reddish belly. The Northern Fur Seal has a short face. **(150)** The **Guadelupe Fur Seal** (not shown) of southern California is similar but has a longer snout.

California Sea Lion This is the "seal" so often seen at circuses and aquariums performing tricks. It is a very noisy barker. This sea lion swims at speeds of up to 25 mph. Its home is the California coast. Some of the males wander up to Canada. Both males and females have a high forehead. Males weigh up to 600 pounds. **(151)**

Northern Sea Lion An enormous yellow-brown sea lion with a low forehead. The males weigh up to 2000 pounds and give lion-like roars. This sea lion is found along the Pacific Coast from Alaska south to California. **(152)**

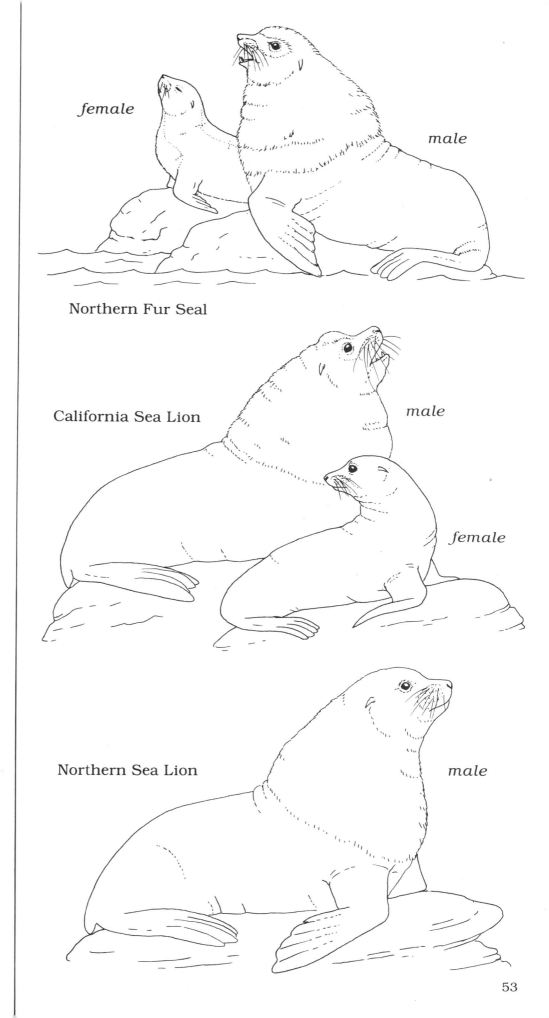

female *male*

Northern Fur Seal

California Sea Lion *male*

female

Northern Sea Lion *male*

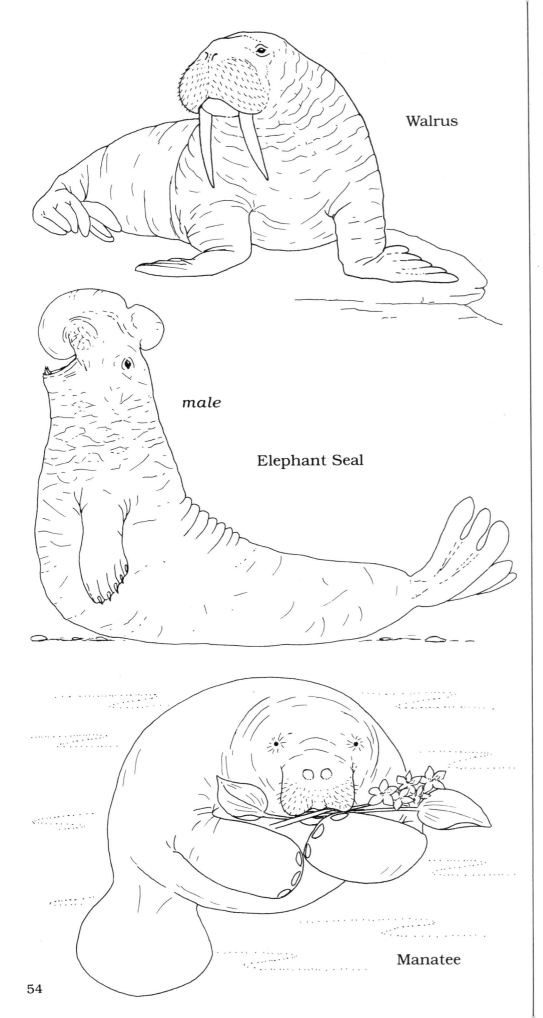

Walrus

male

Elephant Seal

Manatee

Seals

Walrus Both males and females have 2 large white tusks and heavy whiskers. Walruses feed on shellfish, crabs, and small seals in cold oceans of northern Alaska and Canada. Their thick hairless skin is black when wet, pinkish when dry. Walruses can turn their hind flippers forward for "walking," but lack external ears. Males weigh up to 2700 pounds. (153)

Elephant Seal The world's largest seal — males weigh up to 8000 pounds. Older males have a short trunk which amplifies their bellows. Elephant Seals live on the Pacific beaches by day, and hunt sharks, squid, and rays at night. (154)

SIRENIANS

An order of tropical mammals that graze on plants along warm reefs, shores, and rivers. Unlike these vegetarians, seals eat fish and sea animals.

Manatee Not a seal, but placed here for comparison. It is a hairless water mammal with front flippers and a broad paddle-shaped tail. Lives in rivers and coasts from Texas to the Carolinas. Manatees eat water plants, not fish. (155)

Seals: Earless Seals

These seals have no visible ears, just an opening. Their hind flippers cannot be turned forward, so they are forced to wriggle on land.

Harp Seal The male is yellowish white with a dark brown head and dark patterns on the back. The young are entirely yellowish white with large black eyes. Harp Seals are found in eastern Canada, migrating with the edge of the ice pack. **(156)**

Gray Seal A large, grayish or black seal with a long muzzle. Found in the Atlantic from Massachusetts northward. **(157)**

Ribbon Seal Males are brownish with beautiful wide buffy rings around the neck and flippers. Females are more grayish, with less distinct rings. Ribbon seals live on ice floes off western Alaska. **(158)**

Harbor Seal The common small seal of harbors and coasts from the Carolinas and California northward. Its color varies from brown to gray, with many small spots. This seal hauls out on beaches and rocks at low tide. **(159)**

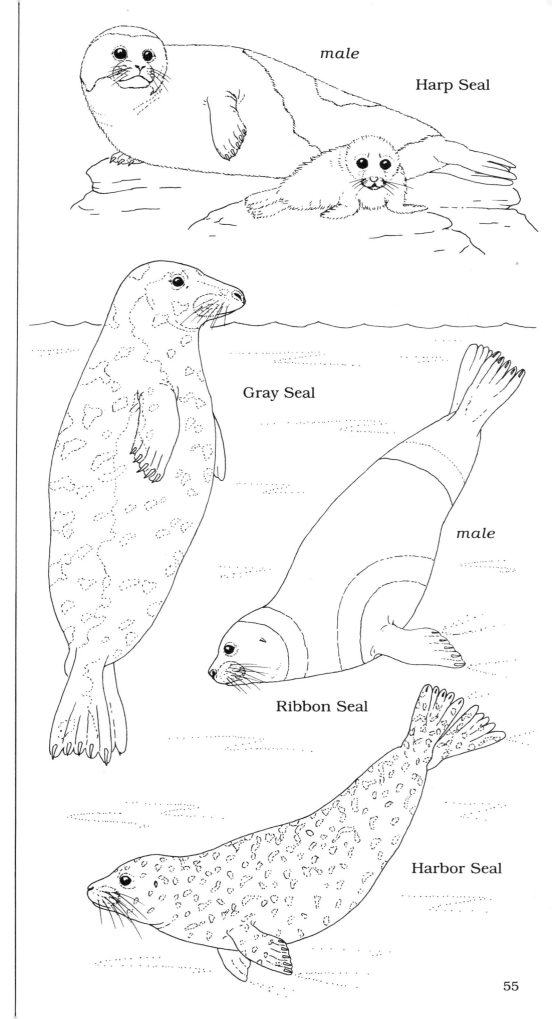

male

Harp Seal

Gray Seal

male

Ribbon Seal

Harbor Seal

HOOFED MAMMALS

Heavy, plant-eating mammals with two toes on each foot (horses have one). In North America we have four native families of hoofed mammals: the deer, which grow and shed antlers each year; the sheep, goats, and Bison, which have permanent hollow horns; the pronghorns, which develop and shed sheaths over their horns each year; and the peccaries.

Collared Peccary A pig-like mammal that roams in bands of up to 25 in the brush and wooded hills of Arizona and Texas. It is gray with a pale neck collar. The Peccary feeds on cactus pads (spines and all), leafy plants, lizards, and snakes. Its tusks point downward. (160) The New World peccaries are in a family distinct from the Old World pigs, because of important differences in foot structure, stomach, and tusks.

Wild Boar An Old World pig, introduced from Europe as a game mammal in New Hampshire, California, and throughout the South. The Wild Boar has long gray hair, but sometimes appears reddish from mud wallowing. Its tail is relatively long and straight, and its tusks point upward. (161)

Collared Peccary

Wild Boar

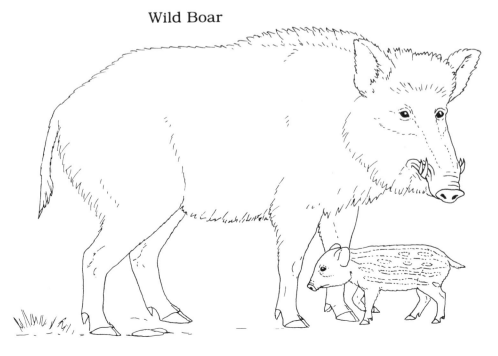

Hoofed Mammals: Deer

The deer family includes the caribou, moose, wapiti (elk), and deer. The males grow new antlers every spring, covered with thin skin and fuzzy hair. Later this "velvet" dries up, leaving hard antlers that are used to battle other males. The antlers drop off during the winter.

"Woodland" Caribou This caribou has brown, shaggy fur and a white neck and mane. Both males and females grow antlers that are flat in places. Their hooves spread out in summer, which makes it easier to walk in bogs. Nearly extinct in the nothern U.S., the Woodland Caribou survives in wilder woodlands of Canada. **(162)**

"Barren Ground" Caribou A very pale whitish race with only a brownish wash on the back. Its antlers are smaller and less flattened than the Woodland's. Huge herds roam the tundra of Alaska and arctic Canada. **(163)**

Elk (Wapiti) A large, dark brown deer with a pale yellowish rump and short tail. Males have a shaggy neck mane and large antlers late in the year. Often seen in groups of several dozen in sheltered meadows of our western national parks. Males weigh up to 1000 pounds. **(164)**

Woodland Caribou

Barren Ground Caribou

male

Elk (Wapiti)

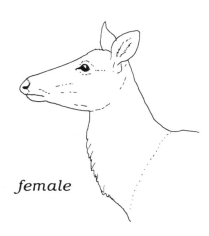

female

Hoofed Mammals: Deer

Mule Deer This deer constantly moves its long, mule-like ears, listening for danger. Compared to a Whitetail it is grayer, has a shorter tail, a thicker neck, a wider face, and black on the tail. The Mule Deer is the most important big game mammal of the West. Mule Deer are regularly seen in most western parks and protected areas, but rarely in large groups. They follow trails and are active day and night. Many summer in high country and winter in valleys. Typical inland Mule Deer have blackish heads with whiter faces and throats. Males weigh up to 400 pounds. **(165)**

"Black-tailed" Deer In the coastal Pacific Northwest forests live 2 smaller races of Mule Deer. They are darker brown and the top of the tail is all black. **(166)**

Mule Deer

male in early winter

male in summer velvet

"Black-tailed" Deer

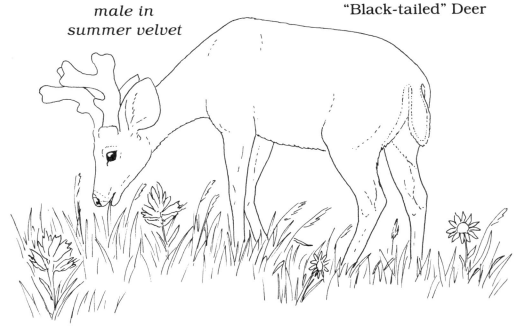

Hoofed Mammals: Deer

White-tailed Deer Glimpses of this deer's "white flag" tail bounding into a forest, or a doe with its white-spotted fawn, are highlights of any day's outing. The Whitetail is reddish brown most of the year, but grayer in winter. This deer is the most important game mammal in the East. It is widespread in woods, swamps, and brush over much of the U.S. and southern Canada. It sometimes becomes too common due to its freedom from predation by wolves and cougars. White-tailed Deer eat twigs, grasses, fungi, apples, and acorns. They are excellent swimmers and adapt well to the suburbs. Unfortunately, they are often struck by vehicles. Active day or night, they can run up to 35 mph, jump 8 feet high, and leap 30 feet in one bound. Small races of White-tailed Deer are found in the Florida Keys and Arizona. Males can weigh up to 400 pounds. **(167)**

female in summer

White-tailed Deer

fawn

male in early winter

59

Hoofed Mammals: Deer

Moose The largest deer in the world. A male Moose may weigh up to 1400 pounds. Every year the males grow massive flat antlers with small prongs. The Moose is dark brown with gray legs, an overhanging snout, a hanging dewlap off the throat, and a shoulder hump. It lives in the great northern forests of Canada, Alaska, the northern Rockies, upper Midwest, and New England. Moose are often seen feeding on water plants in ponds in summer. In winter they feed on bark, twigs, and saplings. The rust-colored youngsters lack spots. **(168)**

Moose

female

male

More Hoofed Mammals

Pronghorn Mistakenly called an antelope, the Pronghorn flashes its white rump as it dashes about the arid plains of the American West at speeds of up to 50 mph. Males have black patches on the face and neck. Unlike deer, the Pronghorn has permanent horns. A sheath grows over these each summer and is later shed. Males and most females have these horns. Pronghorns browse on weeds, sagebrush, and grasses. Pronghorns usually feed and travel in small groups. **(169)**

Bovids

This group of hoofed mammals includes the Bison, Muskox, goats, sheep, cattle, and the true antelope and buffalo of the Old World. Both males and females have unbranched hollow horns that are never shed.

Bison A huge (up to 2000 pounds) dark brown grazer with a high hump on the shoulder. Long shaggy golden or brown hair hangs from the shoulders and front legs. Sixty million were shot on the Great Plains in the 1800s. Fewer than 1000 survived to be rescued by conservationists. This mammal has been erroneously called a buffalo for years. **(170)**

Pronghorn

female

male

Bison

61

Mountain Goat

Muskox

Hoofed Mammals: Bovids

Mountain Goat A yellowish white goat with a throat mane or beard. Its thin black horns curve backward. The Mountain Goat is an excellent climber but a slow runner, so it tends to stay near rocky crags where few predators venture. Its flexible black hooves, compact muscular body, and short legs provide good balance, enabling it to cross very narrow ledges. Small herds inhabit western mountains from Montana to Alaska. **(171)**

Muskox A high arctic denizen that once was a major food item for Eskimos until it was wiped out by hunters with modern rifles. The Muskox is now being reintroduced in Alaska and northern Canada. Its long brown silky fur hangs down nearly to its feet. The broad flat horns curve forward. Muskoxen typically form a "wagon train" circle to face outwards at danger. They stand 5 feet tall, and can weigh 900 pounds. **(172)**

Hoofed Mammals: Bovids

Bighorn (Mountain Sheep) A thick-necked sheep with a creamy white rump. Males have horns that form massive coils, while females have much thinner, pointed horns. Larger and darker brown in the northern Rockies, Bighorns are smaller and pale tan-colored in the desert ranges of the Southwest. Males engage in serious butting contests in fall, making loud noises. (173)

Dall's Sheep This sheep replaces the Bighorn in Alaska and the Yukon area. It is all white with black hooves and large yellow horns that are smaller than those on a Bighorn. Dall's Sheep are commonly seen by visitors to Denali National Park in Alaska. A dark race known as **Stone's Sheep** occurs in western Canada. It can be black, brown, or silver, with contrasting white rump, belly, face, and leg trim. (174)

female

male

Bighorn (Mountain Sheep)

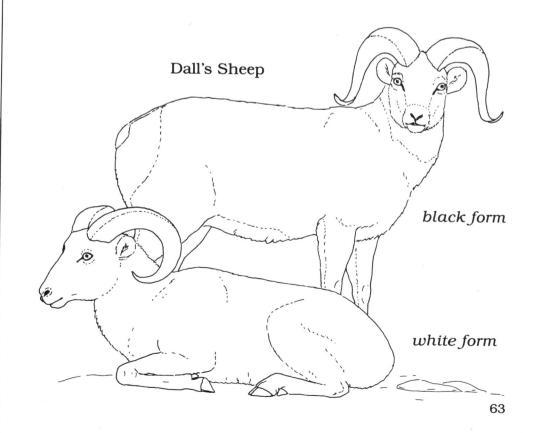

Dall's Sheep

black form

white form

Biomes of
North America

Biomes of North America
Color in the 10 major plant communities of the U.S. (minus Hawaii) and Canada. Mammals, birds, and most other animals are often found in just one or a few of these dominant habitat groupings.
1. Pink: Great Basin, cooler desert scrub, sagebrush

2. Red: Southwestern desert, warmer cactus scrub
3. Orange: Prairie, scrub, and oaks
4. Yellow: Great Plains, grassland with riverine forest
5. Light green: Eastern forest, broadleaf mixed with pine
6. Dark green: Northern and montane forest, mainly conifers

7. Blue: Oceans and Great Lakes
8. Purple: Pacific Northwest, wet coniferous forest
9. Brown: Arctic tundra and alpine grasslands
10. Black: Mexican border woodlands and tropical savanna.

128

129

130

131

132

133

134

135

136

137

138

139

140

141

142

143

144

145

146

147

148

149

150

151

152

153

154

155

156

157

158

159

160

161